W9-BNP-613

THE KING AND THE COWBOY

ALSO BY DAVID FROMKIN

Europe's Last Summer:
Who Started the Great War in 1914?

Kosovo Crossing:
The Reality of American Intervention in the Balkans

The Way of the World: From the Dawn of Civilizations
to the Eve of the Twenty-first Century

In the Time of the Americans: FDR, Truman,
Eisenhower, Marshall, MacArthur, the Generation That
Changed America's Role in the World

A Peace to End All Peace:
Creating the Modern Middle East 1914–1922

The Independence of Nations

The Question of Government: An Inquiry into the
Breakdown of Modern Political Systems

THE PENGUIN PRESS

New York

2008

THE

KING

AND THE

COWBOY

THEODORE ROOSEVELT AND
EDWARD THE SEVENTH,
SECRET PARTNERS

DAVID FROMKIN

THE PENGUIN PRESS
Published by the Penguin Group
Penguin Group (USA) Inc., 375 Hudson Street, New York,
New York 10014, U.S.A. • Penguin Group (Canada), 90 Eglinton Avenue East,
Suite 700, Toronto, Ontario, Canada M4P 2Y3 (a division of Pearson Penguin
Canada Inc.) • Penguin Books Ltd, 80 Strand, London WC2R 0RL, England •
Penguin Ireland, 25 St. Stephen's Green, Dublin 2, Ireland (a division of
Penguin Books Ltd) • Penguin Books Australia Ltd, 250 Camberwell Road,
Camberwell, Victoria 3124, Australia (a division of Pearson Australia Group
Pty Ltd) • Penguin Books India Pvt Ltd, 11 Community Centre, Panchsheel
Park, New Delhi–110 017, India • Penguin Group (NZ), 67 Apollo Drive,
Rosedale, North Shore 0632, New Zealand (a division of
Pearson New Zealand Ltd) • Penguin Books (South Africa) (Pty) Ltd,
24 Sturdee Avenue, Rosebank, Johannesburg 2196, South Africa

Penguin Books Ltd, Registered Offices:
80 Strand, London WC2R 0RL, England

First published in 2008 by The Penguin Press,
a member of Penguin Group (USA) Inc.

1   3   5   7   9   10   8   6   4   2

Photograph credits
Page 69: Maison Soubrier
Page 220: Library of Congress, Prints and Photographs Division
All other photographs: Mary Evans Picture Library

ISBN 978-1-59420-187-5

Book design by Marysarah Quinn

In a New York high school a few years back, it was
observed that the top students, who until then had
been earning straight As, faltered and fell back
during their senior year: the twelfth grade. The
students came to blame their poor performance
during that final year of high school on
some sort of illness; and to this malady
they gave the name senior slump.

CONTENTS

THE KING AND THE COWBOY

PREFACE

IN 1901, the opening year of the twentieth century, two colorful public figures inherited the leadership of the English-speaking countries. They were sworn into office even though they were generally regarded as not really fit to rule. One was thought to be something of a wastrel; the other, something of a clown.

But once in office, they gave evidence of possessing impressive qualities. Moreover, behind the scenes they worked together. Outside of a select circle, it was not known at the time—indeed it is not widely known even today—but King Edward and President Roosevelt became something like political partners. Moved in no small part by the two, the political structure of the globe was turned upside down in the early 1900s as they sought to dispel the shadow cast over world affairs by Germany's Emperor William II. They were among the authors—among the shapers—of our world and would set the stage for much that would occur in the century to come.

WHAT WE ARE ABOUT to see is the birth of the special relationship between America and England—and of the intimacy between England and France.

PART ONE

VICTORIA'S WORLD

1 | WHEN GERMAN MONARCHS RULED ENGLAND

As AN INFANT she was named Alexandrina Victoria. As a child she was known as Drina. As the longest-reigning monarch of the United Kingdom of Great Britain, Wales, and Ireland, she was the Queen Victoria who became Empress of India. Nowadays nobody thinks of her as German, even in part. She is remembered as Englishness incarnate. Yet she was the child of a German family.

Born at dawn on May 24, 1819, she was a child of victory. Only four years earlier, her country finally had defeated its longtime rival, France, though France was led by one of the greatest generals in history, Napoleon Bonaparte. Although Britons could not have known it at the time, the French threat to British security, which had arisen at least a thousand years before, was over at last. The way was clear for the British Empire—Victoria's Britain—to dominate the world.

It was an exciting century over which Victoria presided and in which Britain rose to supremacy. Maritime power, which had played a key role in the defeat of France and in the earlier acquisition of such huge territories on the far side of the world as Australia, Canada, and India, transformed the tiny British Isles into a nation that girdled the globe. Britain's fleet, the Royal Navy, ruled the waves of all the planet's oceans, including the almost unimaginably vast Pacific.

Britain had played a leading role in starting the Industrial Revolution: one of the mere handful of profound changes in human affairs that had occurred since people invented agriculture and moved from caves into houses. The shift to an industrial economy had transformed almost everything—how we live, how we work, how we think, how we dress, how we act. Until the Industrial Revolution the only energy sources available to the human race were the muscles of humans and animals and the harnessing of winds and waves. The release of steam energy and then of other forms of mechanical energy opened up hitherto undreamt-of prospects of wealth and power. Electricity lit up the world and moved the world. Britain, the world's preeminent trading, investing, and colonizing power, was at a point in history where the great expansions came together, and where something new and improving or bigger and better seemed to happen every day. The Victorian era was an age of conspicuous progress that also *believed* in progress—trusted that it would keep on going—and had faith in reform and in the advance of civilization. It bequeathed to us much that we take for granted: such creations as bicycles, photographs, postage stamps, plastics, subways, and traffic lights. The Queen lived the life of her time, welcoming new experiences as they became available. In 1842, for the first time, she traveled by train. In 1847, she went swimming in the sea. Personal experience led Victoria herself to especially value the invention of chloroform for use in childbirth; she had many children—nine in all.

. . .

IN THE TIME of the Hanoverians—the dynasty to which Victoria belonged—the throne of England had become one of the world's great prizes. But to gain it took more than just being conceived by the right sperm in the right womb in the right order.

Britain's rulers in the late 1700s had constructed an obstacle course by way of requirements of eligibility for the throne. The English government at that time had defined by statute which marriages and births and other qualifications enabled a candidate to qualify for elevation to the throne, and in what order. These rules helped to explain why Britons—a people who themselves exercised sway over much of the rest of the world—continued to be governed by a dynasty of Germans from a minor principality called Hanover.

IT WAS THE RESULT of religious conflict. The English, having beheaded a Roman Catholic monarch—Charles I—after the lapse of a century had imported a new king from reliably Protestant Hanover and had crowned him as George I. Not only was he himself German, and not only was he ruler of the German principality of Hanover, he also was married to a German wife and kept two German mistresses. He ruled Britain (1714–1727) for thirteen years without ever learning to speak or understand the English language.

George II, who succeeded his father and ruled Britain from 1727 to 1760, was in turn succeeded by George III, under whose reign (1760–1820) the War of the American Revolution was fought. In turn his son was crowned in 1820 as George IV. George I, II, III, and IV all married Germans. Germany at the time was fragmented into about three hundred principalities and similar units; it therefore had an abundance of Protestant princes and princesses. British royalty, and their cousins throughout Europe, routinely sent to Germany for spouses.

One of the most important functions of rulers in those long-ago days of crowns and castles was to produce recognized heirs. George III did his duty; he and his wife produced fifteen children. George IV produced only one: a *girl*. The lovely Charlotte, Princess of Wales, proved to be a popular heiress-apparent to the throne. At the age of twenty-one, she shared that popularity with the handsome German prince she had married, Leopold of Saxe-Coburg-Saalfeld. But then she died in childbirth, and her baby died too, stillborn.

A succession crisis opened. The king had six bachelor brothers, most of whom were a bad lot: dissolute and deeply in debt. All were loath to marry an eligible aristocrat, but needed the money that a claim to the throne would provide. With heavy hearts, they bowed to circumstances, and German princesses were duly sent for to wed and bed. The race was on.

Victoria's father, the Duke of Kent, won the great prize for her, though he did not survive to enjoy it himself. The reigning monarch— he who was to become George IV—hated Kent and, above all, his German wife: "too German, too fond of Germany, too closely surrounded by German relatives and retainers . . ."[1]— a woman who had to have her "speeches written out for her in phonetic English: . . . ei em most grêtful."[2] The hatred deepened when Victoria's father died soon afterwards, leaving her in the care of her German mother. Victoria was three years old before she began to learn English—as a second language.[3]

. . .

UPON THE DEATH of her uncle King William IV, the heir of the four Georges, Victoria, not far removed from girlhood, was crowned monarch of the United Kingdom on June 28, 1837. She was nineteen years old, and as soon as the ceremony was concluded she ran upstairs and gave her spaniel a bath.

She was well aware that among the adults with whom she mingled there were many, including her mother, who would wish to use her for their own ends. But she was stubborn and not easily led. There were few to whom she was willing to give her trust; chief among them was her Prime Minister, the worldly Lord Melbourne. It was a happy choice, for he was wise and experienced.

The chief duty expected of her was that she marry and start a family. A year after mounting the throne, she told Melbourne, in the words of one biographer, "that the very subject of marriage was odious to her, and that if possible she would prefer never to marry at all."[4] The pressures upon her, however, were too powerful for even Victoria to resist. Relatives had lobbied for a long time for Victoria's marriage with the German Prince Albert of Saxe-Coburg-Gotha. Albert was her cousin. He was handsome, charming, strong-willed, serious, and strong-minded. He came to England to get to know her; and Albert, she confided to her diary, was "*beautiful.*" After consulting Lord Melbourne as to the proper procedure, she proposed marriage to Albert, and he accepted.

Victoria married Albert on February 10, 1840. Their brief honeymoon was spent at Windsor Castle, a royal residence outside London. The honeymoon was a decided success. Victoria wrote in her diary, "I NEVER NEVER spent such an evening!!! My DEAREST DEAREST

DEAR Albert sat . . . by my side, and his excessive love and affection gave me feelings of heavenly love and happiness I never could have *hoped* to have felt before."⁵

Understandably, Victoria hoped to postpone starting a family: for one thing, childbirth, as noted earlier, was dangerous in those days. Moreover, after having experienced honeymoon joys, she wanted to have Albert to herself for a while. She said that she wanted to have one year of "happy enjoyment" with Albert."⁶ It was not to be; she became pregnant almost immediately.

To Victoria's surprise, the delivery was easy. The child turned out to be a girl, but with a rush of confidence she did not care: "Never mind," she said, "the next will be a Prince."⁷

VICTORIA WAS TO BECOME the longest-serving monarch of Great Britain. On May Day 1876 she also became Empress of India. She was less than five feet tall, pudgy, and weak-chinned; but she was forceful and opinionated. She took her duties to family and to country—which she seemed to regard as one entity—with the greatest seriousness. She would have nine children, forty grandchildren, and eighty-seven great-grandchildren; and she devoted a major portion of her time and attention to their marriage alliances. What she wove was a web of influence and control over the Continent by placing her family members in Europe's royalty—at a time when, arguably, monarchs still ruled the world, or at least wielded decisive influence in the governments of nations. The last of her great-grandchildren was still alive in 1930, when some kings still reigned.

She adored and admired her husband, but at first, to a large extent, excluded him from policymaking. In this she seems to have reflected the suspiciousness of the British public, which worried that as a foreigner he might be loyal mainly to his German homeland. It was not until the Great Exhibition of 1851, which Albert helped organize, and the opening of the Crystal Palace that he began to be fully appreciated, both by Victoria and by others. Intended to show Britain's superiority in science, industry, and trade, the Great Exhibition celebrated the peace and prosperity that had flourished in the Victorian era. In 1857 Albert at last was awarded by Victoria the title he should have held all along: Prince Consort. Only four years later, on December 14, 1861, as he was coming into his own, he died, generally worn out and wracked with a disease believed by some to be typhoid.

In Lytton Strachey's imaginative account of the Prince Consort's death, Victoria "shrieked—one long wild shriek that rang through the terror-stricken Castle . . . "[8] The Queen went into a seclusion that lasted for almost three decades. With Albert no longer at her side, she came to rely more heavily on the prime minister of the day. The unintended effect was to move Britain towards a monarchy that was constitutional—despite Victoria's own inclination towards personal rule. And a constitutional rule meant government by politicians, who were thoroughly British, rather than by royals who still were mostly German.

2 | A LIBERAL GERMAN'S WORLDVIEW

OF VICTORIA'S PRINCE CONSORT, we are told that "one of Albert's favorite phrases was 'Ich habe einer plan'—I have a plan."[1] Insofar as he possessed a world-vision, it was to move his plan forward. To a growing extent he was able to contribute to Victoria's policy decision-making even before the opening of the Great Exhibition; and to that extent he was able to bring his distinctive qualities—his virtuous character, his high standards, his methodical approach to issues, and his orderly cast of mind—to the conduct of public affairs.

The same qualities were even more in evidence in family affairs, in which, from the start, Victoria allowed him to participate fully. He was an especially playful and loving father to his first child, Vicki, who was named for the Queen, whom posterity came to identify with the phrase "We are not amused." Vicki was his firstborn, and everything about her was new to him. With her he could indulge the childish side of his nature, which he kept hidden beneath his sober and severe exterior. Vicki made it easy for him; she was ahead of her years, bright, and quick; and she went out of her way to please her parents.

Long before Vicki was ready for it, she was assigned a key role in the world policy of her parents. The international politics of Victoria and Albert, it will be remembered, were family oriented. They married their children in such a way as to promote German liberalism—their own political faith—and the national interests of British foreign policy. So, at the age of fourteen, Vicki, though physically and emotionally still a child, was engaged to marry, Prince Frederick of Prussia: "Fritz," who was in line to inherit the Prussian throne in Berlin.

Albert had trained Vicki in politics, preaching his philosophy of constitutional government. It was through Vicki, who would one day be queen of powerful Prussia, that Albert and Victoria would cement Anglo-German friendship and would reform the continent of Europe along liberal lines and under the leadership of what might become a de facto Anglo-German alliance. That was Albert's plan.

Liberalism in its Continental sense, such as Albert apparently preached, is believed to have begun with Spanish rebels in the first half of the nineteenth century. They, and similar groups elsewhere in Europe, adopted as their program the limitation of power. They demanded that kings should subscribe to a constitution: that not even monarchs, in other words, should be able to exercise unlimited power. The essence of a constitution is that it defines the limits on everyone's power.

Under such statesmen as Canning and Palmerston, Great Britain had championed this political philosophy in the first half of the nineteenth century. In advocating it, Germans such as Prince Albert in effect were proposing that their countrymen should become more like Englishmen.

The importance that Albert attached to imbuing his children with his political faith was not unusual in his time and place. The nineteenth century, driven largely by the Industrial Revolution, was an age of ideology. Other than liberalism, these ideologies included nationalism, several varieties of socialism, and even unregenerate royalism: a continuing belief in the divine right of kings. These views were not held lightly. There were years, such as 1848, when Europe was convulsed by revolutionary fevers; when barricades were erected in the capital cities behind which insurgents sought to overthrow their governments; and when partisans risked their lives for their political creeds.

For Queen Victoria, gaining the tie with Prussia for her royal family must have seemed to be a triumph of the family she led. For her side, she had won the most glittering prize in Europe. For the Prince Consort, it must have seemed to be even more than that and even more than the achievement of a plan that was his; it must have placed the dream of an enlightened world almost within reach. But would Fritz and Vicki's male child, when they had one, follow it through? Would Victoria and Albert's male heir prove capable of realizing his part in it? For, in Victoria and Albert's vision, their eldest son too was to be the champion of their cause.

IN CONTEMPLATING a potential combination of Great Britain and Prussia in the mid-1800s, it is important, however, to put the two in perspective. Prussia was only one of thirty-nine German states at the time, albeit the most dynamic of them. "Germany" was no more than a geographical term.

Great Britain, though composed of four nations—England, Scotland, Ireland, and Wales—was one state: the United Kingdom.

As an industrial power, it dwarfed all others. It produced two thirds of the world's coal; half of its iron; five sevenths of its steel; and 40 percent, in all, of its manufactures. Of all the exports of all the countries in the world, one third went to the British market. And Britain had more steamship tonnage than all the other countries combined.[2]

The combination that Victoria and Albert had in mind was a formidable one indeed.

3 WAS BERTIE REALLY BORN LUCKY?

VICTORIA WAS A PERSON of decided views. She seems not to have noticed how often her expectations were belied. Had she noticed she might have been disappointed less often; for her life was punctuated by disappointments.

She did not know—indeed she could not have known—that hidden deep within her lay the seeds of a dangerous affliction. Though she did not suffer from hemophilia herself, she was a carrier of the deadly disease. Her genetic legacy to her family was tainted. To a large extent she provided Europe with its royal families—but at the same time, physically, she undermined European royalty.

She also did not foresee that she would conceive a second child almost immediately after the birth of the first. It made her angry. She knew that in her day, age, and country the principal duty of a monarch was to produce as many legitimate heirs to the throne as possible— preferably male; and she went further by producing a brood of heirs to other European thrones as well. Yet she did not want to give birth to so many so quickly; and felt that she was being rushed.

Because Vicki's birth had been relatively quick and easy, Victoria imagined that the rest of her confinements would be easy too. She was in for a bad surprise. The future Edward VII was born November 9, 1841, only after "severe labor."[1] It was five or six years before James Simpson began to use chloroform to mitigate the pains of childbirth. There was no anesthetic to help Victoria get through it. Of all her nine children, the future King caused her the most suffering in childbirth. According to one of Edward's principal biographers, she never forgave him for that. He was an unwanted child—in the sense that she did not want him when he came and how he came.

Victoria described him (to her uncle, King Leopold of Belgium) as "a wonderfully strong and large child with very large dark blue eyes, a finely formed but somewhat large nose and a pretty little mouth."[2]

As the oldest daughter was named Victoria after her mother, but then was called Vicki to distinguish her, so the oldest son was named Albert after his father—Albert Edward, to be exact, and Queen Victoria insisted that the "Albert" come first—but he was called Bertie so that people could tell them apart. On December 4, 1841, Queen Victoria appointed her newborn son Prince of Wales. Of the nine children Victoria and Albert were to have, Bertie was not the one the Queen would have chosen to be her heir.

Vicki—little Miss Perfect, as we would call her today—easily won all the races. Bertie, her backward little brother, lagged far behind. How happy the royal family would have been had Vicki, instead of Bertie, been the boy! As it was, Vicki displayed the usual sibling rivalry; she was "not at all pleased with her little brother."[3]

Members of the royal family were expected to behave with decorum, and in large part did so; but it is clear that Bertie's failure to match either his sister's successes or his parents' standards gave rise to lifelong tensions, despite his affection for her and for other members of his family. The tensions were not always apparent, but they must always have been there, like submerged mines stretched across maritime straits of strategic importance, ready to explode if inadvertently touched during an attempted passage.

DESTINY HAD PLAYED one of its unfunny jokes on Bertie. To the outside world, he seemed to have been born the luckiest person on earth. He was born rich and famous; and he lived a life in which he won games and races. An Alexander or a Genghis Khan had to win battles to acquire his conquests, but Bertie simply was going to be *given* his empire—and it would be larger than any empire that the world had known. All he had to do in order to possess it was to be born—though his mother believed that he was clumsy and untalented even at that. His family brought him up in a castle a thousand years old. His country would give him wealth, palatial residences, and, eventually, a large income. His fleets patrolled the world's oceans, which constituted 70 percent of the globe; and of the remaining land surface and its inhabitants, fully a quarter eventually would belong to him or his family. Almost any woman he desired would agree to be his, and he enjoyed to the fullest the pleasures that they afforded him. He could make his views known on any subject he chose, in the sure knowledge that they would be given serious consideration. He could make the acquaintance of anybody in the world, no matter how eminent, and enjoy that person's company, conversation, and friendship. A map of trade routes published during his reign illustrates the wealth of products that the world made available to him: animal furs—fox, bear, seal, and otter—"brought from the shores of Canada's Lake Athabasca by canoes in summer and dog sleds in winter; cochineal, indigo & vanilla from central America;

teak and bamboo from Siam; cinnamon & pearls from Ceylon; tortoise shells & birds of paradise from New Guinea . . ."[4] and much, much more. As the world would see in the course of his life, when he bought racing stables, his horses won the Derby.

He could (and did) drink the world's greatest wines and dine on the creations of the world's greatest chefs; and he was blessed with the large, healthy appetites and strong constitution that enabled him to appreciate them. He could realize almost any ambition, even an ambition to improve the world—whatever he might mean by improvement.

To be lucky is to be awarded the prize without deserving it; indeed without even competing for it. If we were to be granted one wish, luck might be the one for which we would ask—but that, if Bertie's example offers any guide, might well prove to be a mistake. It may be hidden, but luck nonetheless often comes with a price. In Bertie's case, that price was the upbringing planned for him by his parents in order to fit him for all the responsibilities that would fall upon his shoulders along with the gifts. According to Prince Consort Albert, "the welfare of the world" depended upon "the good education of Princes."[5] Every moment of their education was to be mapped out for them.[6] No moment could be wasted. The aim of the education of the royal child was to make him a clone of his father.[7]

It was only because Bertie had the luck to be designated Prince of Wales that he was forced to suffer through an upbringing that he found to be sheer torture. Irony was to be the theme of his life—as it is the theme of history.

PART TWO

A PROFILE OF BERTIE

4 | NEMESIS STRIKES

ALBERT, THE HIGH-MINDED Prince Consort, "had a plan."[1] It concerned Bertie. He shared the plan with his wife Queen Victoria. It was an educational and character-building program that would be designed specifically for Bertie, and imposed upon him, and in the end would make the young Prince of Wales superior to other mortals. He would be made "good and pure."[2] He would be brought up on the strictest moral principles.[3] In the words of Bishop Wilberforce, perhaps the outstanding prelate of the Victorian age, and its spiritual guide, Bertie would be trained to be "the most perfect man."[4] This involved a good deal of abstinence for the unsuspecting child; for Albert, who was upright and humorless, "looked upon pleasure with distrust." Suave Lord Melbourne, a voice from the unregenerate past, warned that "this damned morality will ruin everything."[5] And from young Bertie's point of view, it did.

The young prince was to be educated along lines worked out by Baron Christian Stockmar, a German physician who earlier had helped to educate Bertie's father and who, like the Prince Consort, came from Coburg. Stockmar allowed a baby no rest after emerging from the womb. "A man's education," he wrote, "begins the first day of his life."[6]

German was Bertie's native language, as it was that of his sister Vicki, and as it had been that of the British royal family during a half-dozen reigns. Bertie also spoke French perfectly. By the age of six, he also had mastered a third language—English—though some detected a slight accent when he spoke it.

Languages, however, were Bertie's only accomplishment. He had great difficulty in reading and in learning—difficulties that today might have been ascribed to dyslexia or to attention deficit disorder[7] or to some other disability that we can now help students overcome. But no such helping hand was extended to Bertie.

The young Prince of Wales was not enrolled in Eton or some other of the outstanding boys' schools of his time. His parents feared that if he were, he might be contaminated by association with his contemporaries. Instruction was supplied by private tutors. He was forbidden the company of boys his own age except for structured encounters at which his father or other authority figures, were in attendance.

In Bertie's education, little allowance was made for recreation. His schedule of studies lasted seven hours a day, six days a week. The Sabbath afforded him respite,[8] as did family and other holidays. Albert's education of his eldest son was rigorous, but that provided by tutors proved to be more understanding and less exacting. Henry Birch, the first of the tutors, arrived when Bertie was seven and a half years old. He found the young Prince charming as a person but "extremely disobedient, impertinent . . . and unwilling to submit to discipline."[9] Frustrated by the demands that were made upon him—and that he could not meet—Bertie was subject to violent fits of rage during which he threw things, broke things, and smashed things.

The Prince of Wales was imprisoned by the imperatives that had been imposed by his parents and his instructors and that seemingly flowed from his birth. Those charged with educating him and with forming his character felt constrained too; thus Birch, who decided to resign as tutor, "felt trapped 'morning, noon and night' in the company of a child."[10]

When Bertie was only four years old, the governess to the royal family reported—accurately—that he was "uncommonly averse to learning" and given instead (as it turned out over the next half century) to "enjoyment of life."[11]

How to educate a prince is a subject that has fascinated philosophers at least since the time of classical Athens. In practice it has been attempted by some of the greatest of thinkers, beginning, perhaps, with Plato, with Xenophon, and with Aristotle in the fourth century B.C. In the Victorian age a prospering middle class in the English-speaking world took their turn in imagining how to develop the minds and bodies of their own children. The creation of such schools as Thomas Arnold's Rugby in the United Kingdom and Endicott Peabody's Groton in the United States was the result. They set standards for their pupils that were not always realistic. Their failure, perhaps, at least as exemplified in the upbringing of the Prince of Wales, was in not tailoring the education to the student. Bertie spent time at both Oxford and Cambridge without graduating from either one, and served briefly in the armed forces of his country without learning how to command military formations in their various movements.

His despairing father complained, "Unfortunately, he takes no interest in anything but clothes, and again clothes."[12] But one of his biographers tells us that "he was already a first-class dancing partner and proved to be an amusing dinner companion."[13] For someone who was to spend fifty years as the leader of English society, these were not, perhaps, unimportant accomplishments.

5 SEDUCED BY PARIS

IN THE YEARS following the wars of the French Revolution and of the French Emperor Napoleon I—in other words, the years after 1815—the shadow of Russia fell over Europe. The czars and their reactionary allies helped suppress the forces of constitutional liberalism and of nationalism throughout Europe. Russia also threatened the viability of the Ottoman Empire and, with it, England's road to India, and thus the British Empire itself. Clashing on a variety of issues that ranged from freedom of thought to freedom of trade, the English grew to detest the Russians in the nineteenth century. Not surprisingly, therefore, the two empires found themselves on opposite sides of a war by the middle of the century. France, ruled now by the liberal monarch Napoleon III, Bonaparte's nephew, was Britain's ally in this so-called Crimean War (1853–1856). The two nations, England and France, almost always had been enemies in the past. Now they were allies in Europe.

Neighbors, siblings, and rivals, England and France had grown to nationhood by struggling against each other. That had been true at least since A.D. 1066, when the Norman French crossed the Channel to invade and occupy England. From the time of Louis XIV in the 1600s until the fall of Napoleon (1815), the British had led the coalitions of Continental countries that had taken a stand against French expansion. The wars had ended by exhausting and depleting France. The Crimean War was the last conflict among the Great Powers of Europe in the nineteenth century that France would win. The era of France's hegemony was over in Europe. The French did not know that—not yet. Nor did the British, who, at times, feared France still.

IN THE SPRING of 1855, Louis Napoleon, the Emperor of the French, who styled himself Napoleon III, and his Empress, the dazzling Eugénie, came to Britain on a state visit that celebrated their empires' new friendship and their defeat of Russia. Eugénie wore the latest Paris fashions. She sported crinolines: skirt linings that had just come into vogue in the 1840s. She set out to charm Britain's royal children and succeeded. Longing to give birth to a child of her own, she showered attention on Britain's royal family.

The spring visit by the French was reciprocated in the summer of 1855 by Victoria and Albert, who brought with them their eldest children, Vicki, and fourteen-year-old Bertie. The children, in particular, were overwhelmed. The City of Light was illuminated in every way, as the French capital set out to charm and, indeed, to seduce. France needed an alliance with the United Kingdom in order to pursue its policies elsewhere in Europe. A half century later, it could be understood that the cause of the alliance was advanced in part on that state visit in 1855. It was advanced in the heart and in the mind of the adolescent Prince of Wales.

Napoleon and his city planner Baron Haussmann were ushering Paris into a glorious new age. They were building monumental structures and wide boulevards. There was air; there was light; there was color. They were constructing a new Rome on the banks of the Seine. There was nothing like it.

"What must have overwhelmed [Bertie] was the sudden contact he made, not simply with another city and another country," writes one of his biographers, "but with a totally new way of looking at life, and of living it."[1] Theater, art, music, and nightlife flourished: excitements of all sorts were everywhere. The lovely young ladies of the French imperial court wore deeply plunging necklines; when they curtsied to Bertie—bending low—the vision was one that the fourteen-year-old boy seems to have found overwhelming.

From the prudish austerity of Windsor Castle to Paris, a glittering city out of a fairy tale, where every moment is a festival and the sky each night seems to be lit up by fireworks, was a short distance in miles but, in other ways, a long way indeed; no wonder that Bertie and Vicki asked the French rulers to adopt them and let them stay on in Paris. But your parents would miss you, said the Empress Eugénie. No they wouldn't, replied Bertie and Vicki; they have a half-dozen more like us back home.

6 SEDUCING THE NEW WORLD

BERTIE'S TRIP TO FRANCE when he was fourteen was a major experience in his life. His voyage to North America, when he was almost nineteen, was another.

The tour was Albert's idea, and it was designed to accomplish a number of things at once. Queen Victoria had received several invitations to visit Canada. One was to preside over a new railroad bridge; another was to lay a foundation stone for the new Parliament Building in Ottawa. Inaugurations and dedications of this sort are the everyday work of members of the royal family today. It was prescient of the Prince Consort to foresee the need to integrate the activities of the monarchy into the commemoration of public works.

Queen Victoria was, even before she became widowed, very much a stay-at-home person; she declined all invitations to visit Canada herself. Albert, of course, stayed close to home too. But Bertie, who had been shifted from one unsuccessful educational venture to another, had time on his hands. So Victoria reluctantly agreed to Albert's plan that the Prince of Wales should go in her place. Canada was seized with excitement. The *New York Times* reported it from Quebec:

> Painters, paper-hangers and upholsterers are busy all over the Province of Canada furbishing up brick houses into palaces as sumptuous as possible. Railway Companies are building and gilding cars of state. Municipalities are voting dollars by the thousand for decorations, illuminations, fireworks and balls. The Government is engaging cooks, buying plate, wine and horses, putting a small navy of tugboats into commission, and corresponding with everybody in general. The people are saving up their spare cash to have a glorious and universal "spree." The occasion of the whole is, of course, the approaching visit of the Prince of Wales.[1]

On learning of the planned visit, the President of the United States, James Buchanan, quickly invited Bertie to visit the United States too. Buchanan had served as the U.S. Minister in London; had devoted himself to shoring up Anglo-American friendship; and now seized the chance to solidify the relationship between the two independent English-speaking countries. In turn, Victoria and Albert also were anxious to improve relations with the United States. So it became clear that Albert's plan suited everyone; and arrangements were made under the supervision of the Duke of Newcastle, Britain's relevant Cabinet minister.

On July 10, 1860, Bertie's voyage began. He had boarded the steamship *Hero*, which was harbored in the English Channel seaport of Plymouth. It was the same seaport—the same Plymouth—from which the Pilgrims had embarked to colonize the New World more than two centuries earlier. In a sense, the Prince's voyage validated theirs.

Hero steamed across a summer ocean. Bertie was slightly seasick the first few days, but soon recovered. About two weeks after setting out, *Hero* reached the shores of Newfoundland and Nova Scotia.

Under the headline THE PRINCE OF WALES AT HALIFAX, the *New York Times* on Monday, July 30, 1860, reported:

> The Prince of Wales landed here to-day at noon. The squadron was off the port yesterday. Royal salutes from the fleet and the batteries greeted him upon his arrival, while the people turned out in immense numbers to give him a cordial reception. He was presented with an address at the dock-yard.
>
> He wore the uniform of a Colonel of the army, and rode on horseback to the Government House. Emerging from the gates of the dock-yard, the procession passed through a double file of troops and volunteers to the Government House. Here were a number of triumphal arches erected in the streets, including CUNARD's arch, with a steamship on the top of it; the Volunteer Artillery arch, built of military trophies, the Mayor's arch, the Archbishop's arch, a very handsome Ecclesiastical arch, the Masonic arch, and a number of other very handsome arches, all of which were beautifully decorated.
>
> On the parade the firemen turned out with a "trophy" fifty feet high, surmounted by a calossal [*sic*] figure holding a hose pipe. Thirty-five hundred children of the

schools also turned out in white and blue, and sang the national anthem, "God Save the Queen."[2]

The following day, the *Times* added:

The ball, last night, was a success. The Prince was present and danced with several ladies.

The Prince has been about town in plain clothes, and has been out early each morning.

To-day he visited the ruins of the Duke of KENT's (his grandfather's) farm, three miles from the city.

The grand regatta came off to-day. The weather was fine, and yachts, fishing vessels, men-of-war boats, whaleboats, and canoes participated. There were also horse races on the Common.

There is a display of fireworks this evening.

The Prince had a reception and *levee* at noon.

The Governor entertained the volunteer officers this evening.

The Prince leaves Halifax by rail to-morrow noon for Windsor and goes thence to New Brunswick. An escort of Artillery and Rifles precede him.

Everything has passed off without serious accident, and the celebration is universally admitted by visitors and natives to have been a credit to Nova Scotia.[3]

Bertie spent the following eight weeks in eastern Canada. There were multitudes everywhere hurrahing and huzzahing. Ticket holders were able to view processions and ceremonies. Afterwards there were so-called levees, at which local notables and elites were presented to the future monarch. Then there was sightseeing. There were excursions to see "Red Indians." Dinners followed; and then balls. Bertie proved himself in the waltzes—which at one time had been considered a shocking step—and other dance steps of the era. The English aristocrats who made up the Prince's entourage neither danced nor mingled, but Bertie generously asked a different partner for every dance. In Quebec, while dancing with a Miss Anderson, he slipped and fell; and she fell on top of him. But he gamely, if somewhat lamely, picked himself up and continued.[4]

On September 20–21, 1860, Bertie and his party crossed over to Detroit to begin the U.S. part of the trip. Theirs was a full schedule. By prearrangement, the Prince traveled in the United States as "Baron Renfrew," a private gentleman. This eased protocol problems in a republican America that remained bedazzled by royalty.

From Detroit Bertie left for Chicago, a typical Midwestern metropolis—a former trading post that had experienced explosive growth. It had been incorporated in 1837 with a population of 4,200. At the time of Bertie's visit, that number had grown to well above one hundred thousand.

Earlier that year, in May 1860, the Republican National Convention had convened in Chicago and had nominated an Illinois candidate, Abraham Lincoln, for President. The Republicans were a new political party, just formed; it was their first national convention; and they assembled in a new ten-thousand-seat convention hall. In the America represented by Chicago, the world was new.

Only a month later, Lincoln was elected President. A month after that, South Carolina withdrew from the Union. The Civil War began. Bertie avoided the opening moves by only a few months.

From Chicago, the Prince's party advanced to St. Louis, Cincinnati, and Harrisburg. By the time Bertie's party reached Cincinnati, he was so exhausted that he fell into a sleep from which he could not be awakened. He slept as the crowds seized for his hands and, failing that, shook his legs.[5]

Then came Washington, D.C. The several days in the American nation's capital were exhausting. A reception was held for him in the White House. Not just one but two banquets were held there in his honor—one of them a dinner for six hundred. According to a contemporary eyewitness, "five sixths of the population of Washington and its suburbs" crowded around near Pennsylvania Avenue to watch fireworks.[6] There were long lines to shake the Prince's hand, but after a half hour, he could shake no longer, and withdrew.

On, then, relentlessly, was Bertie propelled: to Richmond, Baltimore, Philadelphia, and then New York, which even then surpassed other cities. "In the evening," writes an Englishman who was there, "there was a grand torch-lit procession . . . "[7] It was staged by the Fire Department. Some five thousand firemen paraded, wielding engines and apparatus of all sorts, firing rockets, and providing entertainment for the crowds, which, it is said,[8] numbered in the hundreds of thousands.

Completing his trip, Bertie visited West Point, Albany, and Boston before ending in Portland, Maine, to cross the Atlantic once again on his voyage home. In Boston, Bertie showed a sure political instinct by meeting the last living American survivor of the Battle of Bunker Hill: America's rising against Great Britain.[9]

A witness to the royal tour wrote at the time that "the nature of Albert Edward, Prince of Wales, is of a highly sensitive order, and there is a timidity about him which makes him shrink from contact with a large and tumultuous crowd . . . "[10] If so, it is all the more impressive that the adolescent prince should have been able to over-come these feelings. He seemed to glory in the crowds. To Canadians he was their future sovereign. But in the United States, he was something far more egalitarian and twentieth century: he was a celebrity.

He also was someone who had found the resources within him to fill the role his father had envisaged for him: that of a democratic royal figure. He had given signs that he could be the people's king.

7 | CAN SHE FORGIVE HIM?

The Prince of Wales . . . is said to have taken to women lately.
—Henry Adams[1]

IN OLDEN DAYS, matchmaking for royal personalities began practically at birth. Due to the luck of his inheritance—a prize in which his future wife would to some extent share—Bertie was the greatest matrimonial catch of his time, and perhaps of all time. Almost any woman, at least in his special world, would have accepted a proposal of marriage from him. On the other hand, few were qualified to be asked.

The bride-to-be had to be roughly Bertie's age, Protestant, and of the blood royal. In July 1858, King Leopold of Belgium, uncle of both Victoria and Albert and as such a senior adviser to their family, compiled a list of the young ladies whom he found eligible.[2] There were only seven of them. The standout selection, the Princess Alexandra of Schleswig-Holstein-Sonderburg-Glücksburg, was Danish and only thirteen, too young to marry.

Queen Victoria wanted her son to marry a German, as heirs to the British throne had done since the early 1700s. A few years after Leopold compiled his list, Victoria deputed Vicki, now a German Princess based in Berlin, to inspect German candidates.[3] Vicki's conclusions were much like those of King Leopold's several years earlier: all of the few eligible candidates were German except for the Danish Princess Alexandra. But on other counts, only Alexandra seemed to be genuinely acceptable!

All of these discussions of whom Bertie should marry were conducted without his knowledge.

THE NINETEEN-YEAR-OLD Prince of Wales who had emerged from his unique private education; who, unbeknownst to himself was about to be matched off to someone he had not yet met and indeed whom his family had not yet chosen; and who seems most of the time to have kept his childhood temper under control, at least when dealing with his parents, rebelled most visibly by smoking both cigars and cigarettes to excess—a disgusting habit according to both his mother and his father.

A picture of him as he appeared in his late adolescence was supplied by a contemporary during Bertie's brief and disappointing passage through Oxford and Cambridge: "I fancy the little spirit he has is quite broken, as his remarks are commonplace and very slow . . ." Speculating on the Prince's future, the same observer commented that he "will I suppose eventually settle down into a well disciplined German Prince with all the narrow views of his father's family. He is excessively polite and that is certainly his redeeming quality."[4]

It was at this point in Bertie's life—in his passage from boyhood to young manhood—that there occurred the episode that would prove to be in many ways a defining experience for him. He was subjected to yet another of those attempts to instruct and improve him. This one was to be a military exercise. It was a timely decision because the outbreak of war with the United States was a distinct possibility in the months to come: Great Britain might intervene on the Confederate side of America's Civil War. An invasion of the United States by Canada seemed likely. Bertie was to spend ten weeks stationed with a battalion of the Grenadier Guards, an army unit. He was to learn how to command at each unit level. No instruction, in the event, was actually provided to Bertie, who therefore learned nothing; and his family put it down to his intellectual inadequacies.

THE GRENADIER GUARDS battalion in question was stationed in Ireland, in County Kildare, west of Dublin. Its base there was Camp Curragh. A half century later a so-called Mutiny at the Curragh— more accurately described as an "incident" rather than a mutiny— would inspire headlines in the British press. Without being given any orders, officers serving at the Curragh in March 1914 were asked whether they would be willing to use force to suppress dissent in northern Ireland, from which many of them sprang; and they replied that they would not do so willingly. It was no real rebellion, nor was Bertie's, yet both involved saying or doing what the authorities in London did not want said or done.

In Bertie's case it began with a prank. After an evening of drinking and boisterousness (it would seem), some fellow officers of Bertie's battalion smuggled into camp a woman named Nellie Clifden. She seems to have claimed to be an actress, was well known around the camp, and apparently was a call girl of some sort. The young officers secretly introduced her into Bertie's bed, hid her in it, and left. When Bertie said good night to his friends, therefore, and went to bed, he bumped into what was hidden under the sheets and covers. It was a life-changing surprise.

So far as we know, nobody had yet instructed Bertie about sex. Boys his own age normally would have passed on some information, however distorted or inaccurate, about lovemaking and childbearing; but he had been carefully segregated by his parents from those his own age, and could not even pick up such scraps of gossip and speculation as the adolescent male imagination ordinarily might provide.

According to Queen Victoria's biographer Elizabeth Longford, "It is doubtful whether Bertie had any very clear idea of what was going on. His parents never attempted to have the facts of life elucidated for him and in his later teens he had himself put some hesitant questions to a volunteer counselor."[5]

The naked female body would not have come as a complete surprise to him; he had seen breasts overflowing the low-cut gowns of the young women at the French court. A woman's body below the waist, however, would have been unfamiliar territory to him. Thus it was not unusual for innocent young male Britons in his day to be astonished—and in some cases disillusioned—by their first glimpse of female pubic hair.

What could he have thought of the completely unexpected endearments that suddenly were lavished upon him: he who (at least we suppose) did not know what should be put where, and what happens then? What could he have made of the hitherto unimagined and artful caresses that he, for the first time, experienced; and that he was invited to reciprocate? It is difficult to imagine the episode at the Curragh from Bertie's point of view; difficult even to imagine how he might have described it to Charles Carrington, the officer who seems to have arranged it.[6]

Earlier accounts of the life of the Prince of Wales have suggested that the episode at the Curragh was an isolated event. A recent biographer tells us that this may not have been so: that club-land gossip at the time had it that the Prince was continuing to see Nellie, although that hardly seems consistent with his seemingly sincere contrition.[7] However, Nellie, bragging of her conquest, apparently had increased her value materially in the circles in which she moved.[8]

Sensational rumors of this sort are difficult to keep secret. Before long they reached the ears of Prince Consort Albert. A gossipmonger seems to have brought the news to him. The day after he learned the news himself—November 13, 1861, four days after Bertie's twentieth birthday—Albert told Victoria, supplying merely the broad outline of what had occurred while sparing her (in her words) "the disgusting details."[9]

The disgraced young Prince of Wales was severely lectured by his father. "The past is the past. You have to deal now with the future."[10] So Albert told him, wisely, but then, as people will do, disregarded his own sensible counsel by proceeding again to chastise him for the past. Nellie frequented dance halls; how could Bertie have taken up with her? She was freely being called "Princess of Wales."[11] What if she became pregnant by some other man, but claimed it to be Bertie's child? The case would be tried in the courts. The monarchy would be dragged down.

Fortunately for Bertie, the scandal, though it spread widely, did not reach the public at large. Other news—notably the American Civil War and the likelihood that Great Britain might be drawn into it—overshadowed it. He himself apologized abjectly.

In the light of his later lifelong philandering, it is amusing that he promised Albert that he would never do it again; for in fact, in the course of a lifetime, he did it all the time.

Then there was the impending tragedy of Bertie's father, the Prince Consort Albert. Those with eyes to see observed that some sort of collapse was at hand. In recent years, permitted at last by Victoria to participate in affairs of state, he had thrown himself into them, working too hard and tiring himself too much. Having finally allowed him a role, Victoria burdened him too heavily. His constitution, we now know, was being undermined by disease. He suffered from insomnia, fatigue, and rheumatic pains. He succumbed in December 1861 to typhoid or to stomach cancer, hepatitis, renal failure, or pneumonia; accounts differ even today.

Whichever it was, Victoria believed that it was Bertie's fault. He had killed his father.[12] She told Vicki, "I never can or shall look at him without a shudder . . ." Even before Bertie's "fall"—his eating of the apple—Victoria had much preferred her husband to her son. She had worried that if she died, Bertie would govern using his own judgment rather than relying on Albert's.[13]

Now an even more dangerous perspective had opened up: Bertie might rule without even receiving wise counsel that he might disregard. The solution that she seems to have adopted—and which came close to succeeding—was for her to outlive her son.

Meanwhile, she entered into an unending widow's mourning and adopted two principles as the themes of her reign throughout the last half of the nineteenth century: (1) Victoria's decisions would be arrived at by appealing to the late Prince Albert's authority, as in each case she sought to discern what Albert would have done, and (2) the Prince of Wales was to have no share in government, and as little voice as possible even in governing his own life and affairs. Ten days after Albert's death the Queen told her uncle King Leopold, "MY FIRM RESOLVE, my *irrevocable decision* . . . is that *his* wishes—*his* plans—about *every*thing are to be *my law*! And *no human power* will make me swerve from *what* he decided and wished . . ."[14] Again and again from then on, she would invoke Albert's authority in reaching a decision that actually was her own.

IN THIS RESOLVE Queen Victoria may well have been misleading either the world or herself. It will be remembered that her great predecessor, Queen Elizabeth, grew up at a royal court seething with intrigue, and when she finally mounted the throne she skillfully played off one suitor against another so that no man, by marrying her, could take away some or all of the power that she had clawed to assemble and had hoarded so successfully.

Victoria's case was not entirely dissimilar. In the field of fifteen children descended from King George III and Queen Charlotte, it had been no sure bet that a female child of one of the younger sons would emerge the winner. Once in line for the throne, she had to thwart plots aimed at making her sign away some of the powers: plots perhaps hatched by her mother and her mother's comptroller, Sir John Conroy.

Victoria, even as a teenager, had learned to guard her powers, and not to share them with men—who would assume that they, as men, were better able to govern than was she.

Biographers tell us that Queen Victoria would never forgive the Prince of Wales for his long and painful birth, and would never forgive him for failing to live up to his father's high expectations, and would never forgive him for the Nellie episode, which broke his father's heart and thus contributed to Albert's early death. The situation may have been more complex than that.

It is amusing that Queen Victoria (who reportedly was never amused) encouraged her daughter Vicki to give *her* son independence and responsibility while denying the same to Bertie. Grandparents frequently indulge their grandchildren in ways they would not indulge their own children, so in that may lie the explanation of an apparent inconsistency. Another possible explanation of this motherly advice may be that it was *Vicki's* power the Queen proposed to give away to Willy—not her own.

Victoria seems to have been someone who was determined to exercise personal control to the maximum extent possible. Even during the giddy days of her honeymoon, she excluded her adored husband from government and politics. There were good reasons for doing so: he was a foreigner, a German prince at the time of their marriage, and as such distrusted by the British public. Still, she did exclude him, and showed no sign of inner remorse for doing so, and treated him as businesspeople in our day sometimes treat spouses: not discussing the business with them.

Of course she could not get away with that sort of thing in British politics, where she was dependent upon Parliament for financial support and much else. What happened after Albert's death, therefore, was that Victoria's withdrawal from public life left more and more decisions for Parliament and the Cabinet to make. The power of the monarchy was diminished—although that probably was not her intention. Where politicians could not replace her in the ceremonial aspects of the Crown, Bertie had to take her place by default.

MEANWHILE, with Albert dead, and with no guarantee that Bertie might not damage the monarchy further, what should Victoria do?

There was only one thing to be done: the fallen Bertie must be married at once, and his lusts consigned to licit channels. Discussion of possible wives for him had gone forward even before the Nellie

*Wedding of Edward VII and Alexandra of
Denmark in 1863.*

affair had taken place or become known. These plans now were accelerated.

The candidacy of the seventeen-year-old blond Danish Princess Alexandra moved from odds-on favorite to winner, even though Alexandra (hereafter "Alix") was not German. Among other things, she was pretty: the only one of the seven eligible candidates who *was* pretty. Bertie's luck had held.

Queen Victoria insisted on informing Alexandra's family of the Nellie Clifden affair, but they seemed to accept the explanation that the adolescent prince had been an innocent entrapped. As one of

Bertie's biographers remarked, "Alexandra's family in any case knew they were making a great match, and were the envy of Protestant Europe."[15] But Alix herself saw things differently. To one of Bertie's sisters she wrote: "You perhaps think that I like marrying your Brother for his position, but if he was a cowboy I should love him just the same and would marry no one else."[16]

Victoria formally announced that Bertie and Alexandra would be married March 10, 1863. All decisions were made by the Queen. She allowed Bertie to invite only six friends to the ceremony itself.[17] Alix's immediate family, too, was invited. The marriage took place in a chapel last used for such a ceremony a thousand years before. The Queen took no public part in the festivities because she remained in mourning for Albert—indefinitely.

8 WAR AND POLITICS DIVIDE THE FAMILY

BEFORE THE WEDDING ceremony could take place, Queen Victoria dispatched Bertie, along with Fritz and Vicki, on a borrowed royal yacht for a Mediterranean cruise. The Queen ordered Alix to stay behind and spend several weeks with her. It was to be a sort of orientation course for the teenaged bride-to-be, and Alix was understandably terrified.

Victoria told Alix that in marrying into the British royal family she must transfer her loyalties. She must, as it were, give up her nationality. By this Victoria did not mean that Alix must put England first. She seems to have meant that Alix must put *Germany* first. The interests she would uphold from now on must be those of Bertie's family, not of her own. It was to the House of Hanover—the royal line that led from George I to Victoria—that she now belonged: "The German element has to be maintained . . ."[1]

Keen to certain aspects of political symbolism, Victoria went out of her way to spell out in public—and in particular to the courts of Germany and to the German public—the same message that she delivered to Alix. It was no accident that she forbade Bertie to visit Copenhagen; such a trip might have been construed as a sign of support for Denmark, or opposition to Prussia and the other German states, in the conflict that pitted Danes against Germans at the time. Maintaining the close German connection was Victoria's priority.

IN UNDERTAKING TO REORIENT her future daughter-in-law, Victoria was undertaking to carry out a program of adult education. She and the late Prince Consort already were proven failures at child education. They had both blamed Bertie for that.

The educational failure, as viewed from the vantage point of the twenty-first century, was not Bertie's, but that of Prince Consort Albert. Though Albert modified his design for Bertie's upbringing from time to time, and reorganized the royal classrooms as Victoria produced more and more children, his rigidity and rigor of approach remained. He continued to believe that children could and should be shaped by plan and blueprint. His failure, as seen from a modern point of view, was in overlooking the human factor.

ALBERT'S FAILURE—and Victoria's—extended to their political grand design. They produced a large family of princes and princesses well placed to lead Europe. Their daughter married a prince who became Emperor of Germany, and would (in their design) join the German dynasty and the United Kingdom in leading the English-speaking world and the German-speaking world and the rest of the Continent onto the paths of enlightened constitutional monarchy. As so often was the case, Britain's Queen and her Consort were disappointed. Things did not turn out as they expected. They feared that it might be the failings of their son that would cause their plans to be derailed. Instead it would be due to the machinations of their grandson, Vicki's son, who was to become the German Emperor after his father's untimely death. It was Willy, not Bertie, who derailed their plans.

As noted earlier, Victoria's vision—and the Prince Consort's—was for an Anglo-German combine to spread the enlightened progressive politics of constitutionalism for which German and British liberals stood.

Those politics, however, were being challenged in Germany itself at the time Alix was marrying Bertie in the 1860s. King William of Prussia was engaged in a protracted struggle with his parliament. A complex of issues was involved—the budget, taxes, the shape of the military, and such—but the most important of these was the question of whether the king was bound by the constitution or whether, on the contrary, he could overrule it and the legislature. Ministers and proposals came and went; but in the end—and it was a last resort—King William reluctantly appointed Otto von Bismarck, the reactionary man of "blood and iron," as his chief minister with full powers. Bismarck (born 1815) was a Prussian Junker, a rural landowner of the warrior caste, so proclaimed by his bearing and his dueling scars. In politics he was a loner who had no following, belonged to no party, and had never served as a Cabinet minister. What Bismarck offered to Prussia's monarch was unflinching brutality: he had no qualms. As William's minister and in his name, Bismarck disregarded the constitution and dissolved parliament. Later he decreed an end to freedom of the press.

Fritz, heir apparent to the Prussian throne and Bertie's brother-in-law, repeatedly wrote to his father protesting, but to no avail. Finally he spoke up in public. His father then ordered him to stop making speeches.

Fritz was hailed in England, but reviled in Germany, where he was pictured as having fallen under the influence of Vicki, his English wife. Vicki herself was extremely unpopular in Germany, her adopted country. There may have been something in her personality that gave the impression that she was too used to having her own way. It could have been something that she had brought along from nursery days; she had been her father's favorite, and he had given her regular lessons in principles and politics. Whether at studies or at tests, she had been quick and Bertie had been slow; she had been right and Bertie had been wrong. It would not have been surprising if some aspect of the little Miss Know-it-all had clung to her.

ONE OF THE SIMMERING disputes in European politics pitted the various German states against Denmark's royal duchies of Schleswig and Holstein. Title to them resided personally in the King of Denmark, though Holstein had a large German population. Even Schleswig had a large German element in its population. The death of the Danish King in 1864 opened up the question of succession, which was complex. There were more claimants than one.

"The duchies belong to Papa," Alix insisted.[2] Her father had just inherited the Danish crown, and Alix believed that he had inherited the duchies too. Bertie took her side. After complex diplomatic maneuvering the formidable army of Prussia, allied with that of Austria, marched on the duchies. Denmark expected the other Great Powers of Europe to come to its aid. They did not. Early in 1864, in a brief and decisive military campaign, the German powers conquered the duchies. Among those serving in the forces of the victorious invaders was Fritz; for he and Vicki were trying to show their German nationalism.

Until the 1860s German nationalism had been liberal; for that reason Bismarck, a nationalist but an antiliberal reactionary, had refused to support it. Now he was setting out to fulfill the nationalist program, and his successes in doing so were so dazzling that nationalists let him have his way in suppressing liberalism. Hence Fritz, who had opposed Bismarck on the constitution, now served him in the affair of the duchies. And so a rupture had opened up in Victoria's ruling family: Bertie was breaking with Germany. He was wholeheartedly on the side of his wife and of her family. In the end, Queen Victoria was to conclude that "Alix, as good as she is, is not worth the price we have had to pay for her . . . "[3]

9 | THE YOUNG MARRIEDS

AT LAST, IN THE EARLY 1860S, Bertie started to come into his own. At the age of twenty-one, as was expected in English practice, he was provided with a substantial independent income suitable to his position. He was supplied with two palatial residences: Sandringham in the country; Marlborough in town. He was a married man and, as expected, provided heirs for the throne; but even so the Queen found fault.

Victoria was not entirely pleased with her daughter-in-law, and was less so as time went on. She complained that Alix "has the smallest head ever seen" and added, "I dread that—with the small empty brain—" this defect bodes ill "for . . . future children."[1]

Princess Alice (Countess of Athlone, 1883–1980), last survivor of Queen Victoria's numerous grandchildren, in old age remembered that while Alix was much loved, "being stone deaf and not mentally bright, she was not much of a companion for an intelligent man like Uncle Bertie."[2]

It is curious that with all the premarital vetting that Alix underwent, nobody seems to have looked into the question of her hearing. Alix's mother was somewhat deaf. Alix's hearing was bad and became worse. On the other hand, everybody seems to have noticed her good looks, and seems not to have exaggerated them. Bertie's brother Alfred Edward ("Affie") offered to marry Alix if Bertie was reluctant to do so; and later Victoria noted that she would have to keep him away from the young married couple[3] in order to prevent folly or scandal.

Bertie and Alix's move into their own house—Marlborough House—provided the occasion for the kind of celebrations that the public, until then, had been denied because of Victoria's indefinitely prolonged mourning. The balls, banquets, and partying went on for weeks. Focusing on dress, as he had since childhood, Bertie changed clothes six times a day. For decades to come, he served as monarch of pomp and circumstance, while his mother dealt with matters of state. Great Britain, from the death of Prince Albert on, was led by what was in effect a divided monarchy. Queen Victoria, her ministers, her parliaments, and their civil servants governed; while the Prince of Wales performed the ceremonial functions of office and led society. Although severely criticized for it in the press and by political and social figures, Victoria insisted on remaining in seclusion for almost all the rest of her life, which lasted for four decades. In effect she abdicated her social responsibilities. She presided only over the substantive and policy parts of her job. Yet she must have disapproved of the direction in which society was being taken by Bertie—who, in default, took charge.

As one of his recent biographers has put it, "The Prince of Wales rejoiced in the company of precisely those people who were not admitted in society: actors, Americans, Jews and self-made men."[4] The Marlborough House set, as they were called, were fast and aimed always to be up-to-date—and indeed ahead of the date. They stayed up late, and squandered everything: money, health, youth, and much else. They slavishly followed Bertie's every taste and every whim. He smoked to excess; so did they. He drank to excess; so did they. He gorged on rich feasts; so did they. If they did not follow him in eating five meals a day, it was not for lack of trying—although he was capable of consuming more than ten courses at a sitting. At the racetracks or at the gambling tables he sometimes risked more than he could afford—and so did they. Pranks were popular. Alix tried hard to keep up with Bertie in the round-the-clock partying, but could not; she slept till noon, and almost always was late for appointments. Of course having children slowed her down, but Bertie, easily bored, waited for nobody: in their life together, he habitually left her behind.

Early in their marriage, the pattern was set. Bertie was fiercely loyal to Alix as his life partner and as the mother of his children. He did not hesitate to defend her even against his own mother, the formidable Queen Victoria, and did not allow any criticism of her. That extended to politics. At the outset the Queen had imposed the rule that Alix must transfer her political loyalties from her Danish family to her German in-laws; but Bertie, instead, joined Alix in being pro-Danish and anti-German—especially anti-Prussian.

When it came to sex, however, Bertie had no loyalty at all. Some biographers have speculated that it was because slender, ethereal, graceful Alix—she who had almost no waist, and of whom it was said that she had the best legs in Europe—was frigid: one of those icy blond snow princesses from the north. It seems irrelevant. Bertie was simply someone who, having been deprived for so long, wanted all the women he could get.

A couple of years after marrying Alix, Bertie was sent by his parents on a ceremonial mission to Russia. He was to attend a wedding. Alix, because she was pregnant, could not attend. Bertie, handsome with a newly grown beard that masked his weak chin, took advantage of his liberty. In the words of a biographer, with neither his mother nor his wife to observe him, "The Prince was learning, in both St. Petersburg and Moscow, that he could bed almost any woman he wanted . . ."[5]

10 | OTHER BEDS, OTHER WOMEN

> "*—They order, said I, this matter better in France—*"
> —Laurence Sterne, *A Sentimental Journey*

BERTIE NOW CLAIMED that he could no longer go to sleep at night unless a woman was in bed with him.[1] Of these comforting bed-partners, his wife—six times pregnant—was only one of many.

TO BERTIE, France was a second home. One of his biographers, Gordon Brook-Shepherd, points out that "whereas in Victorian London clever talk centred largely around men's clubs, in Proustian Paris it centred largely around women's *salons*. The Prince could enter into the spirit of any entertainment arranged for him by the Princesses de Sagan, the Comtesse de Pourtalès or the Baronne Alphonse de Rothschild . . ."[2] He was a member of their society.

In France the frontiers among entertainments were blurred. Restaurants such as Maxim's, where one danced and sipped champagne, blended into clubs such as the Moulin Rouge where women kicked high to the cancan in more or less undress. All were bracketed by conversation: from those who led society's salons, through the kept courtesans, to the residents of the fashionable bordellos.

Even in his youth, Bertie had been a handsome man. Bertie's appearance in his late teens, a few years before his marriage, was described in unappreciative terms by his mother Victoria to his sister Vicki, who had not seen him for some time: "He is a little grown . . . but his nose and mouth are much grown also; the nose is becoming the true Coburg nose and begins to hang a little; but there remains unfortunately the want of chin which with that large nose and very large lips is not so well in profile."[3] His eyes remained blue, and they bulged, as Hanover eyes did: they popped.

It was in the first ten or fifteen years of his marriage that Bertie grew into the middle-aged man with whose image posterity is familiar. Living the hedonist life against which his parents had cautioned, he threw himself into the almost unlimited self-indulgence that shaped him.

A fifteen-year-old girl who saw him in Paris at the theater when he was in his early thirties told her diary, "The Prince of Wales has charming manners, but one cannot say that he is good-looking. He is below average height, quite fat, and has a rather beautiful oval face with . . . a short, thick beard and . . . very little hair."

The next day she saw him at a Paris railroad station, the Gare de l'Est, and recorded that the "adorable Prince" was with not just one but two cocottes—prostitutes, or, as one might have said at the time, sporting girls. She added, "That's practically nothing for him—this playboy, this Lovelace, this Don Juan. To be what he is, only to be better loved, and I am altogether certain that he is in every divorce court. Women play around with all kinds of rascals, and wouldn't it be absurd for them to resist such a prince?"[4]

In the first decades of their marriage, the Waleses had six children. Clearly it took a great toll on Alix, who was physically frail. The death of their firstborn, Edy, was a tragedy that brought them together. It was a great blow to both parents, too, when the sixth child survived only for one day.

Bertie was bored whenever the entertainment stopped. Through all the pregnancies, Alix tried to keep up with him and his needs but could not. The games and parties at Marlborough House went on, notoriously, into the late hours, even though Alix needed sleep. She was not quick, and knew that she lost her husband's attention when, for example, their young crowd switched from the old-fashioned card game of whist to the up-to-date game, bridge.

After a time, Alix turned to a love of her own, an officer named Oliver Montague. It seems to have been a platonic affair, but they were soul mates. He was her gallant chevalier. He taught her to fish in the trout streams of the peaceful countryside. His devotion was known and recognized. But he died young. She mourned him but did not replace him.

The Prince of Wales started by chasing actresses and chorus girls. He instructed his private secretary to ask young Lord Rosebery, a future Prime Minister, for the use of his Berkeley Square house for bedding girls from nearby theaters—for his own use, and also that of his younger brother, Affie. Rosebery refused. But slipping across the Channel to Dieppe in France always was convenient, making it possible to carry on in both countries, as Wales did with, among others, Hortense Schneider, the famously well-rounded cancan girl of Offenbach's comic operas.

Bertie's womanizing went through a number of distinct phases. In the earlier days of his marriage, any liaison had to be furtive, with his identity well hidden. As he became more familiar with the high life and low life of Paris and London, presumably he felt more at home in borrowed premises and more at ease seeking pleasures in the gaslit world of the 1860s and thereafter.

The trip to Russia had opened his eyes to other possibilities: to the possibilities offered by diplomatic travel. In any event he would be going on goodwill tours at the request of the British government of the day. He and Alix visited Egypt just before the opening of the Suez Canal. Their party brought along three thousand bottles of champagne, four thousand bottles of claret, and four French chefs for their Nile river cruiser. We are told that while Bertie climbed up the Great Pyramid, Alix "was visiting the royal harems, and spent much of the rest of the visit teasing her husband over the lovely unveiled faces she had seen behind harem doors."[5]

To these semiofficial visits he would add pleasure trips of his own. Toward the end of his life, the excursions abroad for pleasure more and more assumed a fixed character: an annual schedule in which Monte Carlo, Biarritz, and other favorites recur.

He had begun by finding that actresses were easy. He had gone on to discover that Frenchwomen were easy. In the end he learned that—uniquely for a Prince of Wales—all women were easy.

In 1874–1875, Bertie spent much time planning a trip to India. In those days, such a voyage would take months. Bertie kept it a secret from Alix, for he did not intend to take her along: it was to be a sort of prolonged bachelor party.

When Alix found out, she was furious. She insisted on being taken along, and appealed for the support of Britain's political leaders—but to no avail. The India trip, in retrospect, marked the institutionalization of Bertie's life as a single man where sex was concerned. As always, Alix was complaisant. Her objection to being left out was that she badly wanted to make the trip: she dreamed of traveling to India. As long as thirty years later she still was to talk of it. Her biographer Georgina Battiscombe tells us that "a visit to 'that most beautiful and fairylike country' became the unfulfilled ambition of her life, a dream to which she referred over and over again."[6]

Swirling around the India trip were many of the issues that characterized Bertie's tenure as Prince of Wales. To begin with, there was his complete sexual freedom, and, associated with it, his day and night drinking, feasting, gambling, cigar smoking, and partying with a sporting crowd that proper society found disreputable. There were those who were shocked that Alix allowed him to do whatever he wanted in this respect.

Since Bertie would be long gone on his passage to India, Alix decided to take the children and vacation in Denmark. Queen Victoria refused permission, and, as always after Bertie's marriage, the family split along pro- and anti-Denmark factions. Bertie, as usual, supported Alix. Victoria, having decided to open Parliament in person, needed either the Prince or the Princess by her side; with Bertie at sea, it had to be Alix. The ultimate conclusion was that Alix could travel to Denmark, but was to cut the trip short for the opening of Parliament.

While Bertie was in the exotic East, a tangled scandal threatened to erupt, as it did from time to time in the fast set that he frequented. "Sporting Joe" Aylesford was one of his companions in India. From London Aylesford had received a letter telling him that his wife, Lady Aylesford, was having an affair with Lord Blandford, a friend of his and Bertie's. Lady Aylesford and Blandford had been about to elope and to divorce their respective spouses but had been dissuaded by Blandford's brother, who pointed out that social ruin would result. Sporting Joe proposed to return to England and to divorce his wife: a course of conduct of which Bertie approved.

Once again social ruin faced Blandford and Lady Aylesford; to prevent that they decided to blackmail Bertie, forcing him to change sides and to insist that Sporting Joe drop the divorce proceedings. The blackmail was a packet of love letters that Bertie had written to Lady Aylesford at an earlier time when he was flirting with her. Lady Aylesford took these with her in calling on Alix.

"Lady Aylesford" was announced at Marlborough House. Alix would not have received her had she heard the name; but, partly deaf, she did not want to admit that she had not understood. So she had her servants admit Lady Aylesford; and that was how Alix, too, was given an account of the affair and willy-nilly was involved in it. Lawsuits and challenges to duels lent a theatrical aspect to these proceedings until a friend of all parties, Lord Hardwicke, negotiated an agreement that settled matters. Critics of the Prince of Wales were not entirely wrong in saying that during his tenure matters were often on the edge of scandal. He was the first royal person since Henry IV to be called to testify in a court of law: it was suggested that he (and others among his friends) had sexual intercourse with the wife of a Member of Parliament named Charles Mordaunt, and Mordaunt sought a divorce. But the woman in question was unstable; she was not a credible witness, and although there was strong circumstantial evidence against the Prince, he denied it all. He may have been innocent. Still it was widely believed that these were not people that he should have known. Then there was the Tranby Croft case: a messy affair involving illegal baccarat gambling. Again, Bertie may have been innocent.

. . .

BERTIE APPEARED—especially to his long-suffering mother—to have surrounded himself with scandalous acquaintances. One of Bertie's biographers, Keith Middlemas, tells us that the scandals were rife: "The Marquis of Waterford eloped with the wife of his friend, and the heir to Lord Winchlow died in a brothel. Lord William d'Eresby, Joint Hereditary Grand Chamberlain of England, fleeced his mistress of thousands of pounds and then eloped with her maid." There was the revelation that Lord Euston had not only married a woman of low social position, but that she also had turned out to be a bigamist.

One of Bertie's many flashy friends in the extravagant 1860s was the young Sir Henry Chaplin, the son of a railway millionaire. Chaplin was a fixture of the sporting-racing-gambling set to which Bertie was strongly attracted. At a May Ball in the 1860s, Sir Henry fell madly in love with Lady Florence Paget, a wild free spirit, said to be the greatest beauty of the age, whose petite frame led her to be called the Pocket Venus. They met in the spring of 1864 and were to marry in August. But in July she eloped with another man: Chaplin's dashing rival, the fourth and last Marquis of Hastings. All three were in their twenties; and all three were fanatics of the turf. The two young men were mortal rivals in life.

In 1867 Chaplin proposed to enter his horse Hermit in the Derby. A month beforehand the horse burst a blood vessel. Chaplin's shattering defeat seemed certain. Rushing to be in at the kill, Hastings bet on another horse—on the favorite—to win; and he backed his bet with everything he owned.

At the very last minute before the start of the race, Chaplin dashed about, taking every bet he could find on Hermit: Hermit, whose trainer had lovingly cared for him day and night all month long. When the race began, therefore, Hastings had everything he had in the world riding on the favorite, while Chaplin had his bets backing Hermit—at the astonishing odds of 100 to 1 against. The race was run after a snowfall (say some) or during a snowstorm (say others). Hermit won.

Hastings, who had lost everything, died: a suicide, according to some accounts, or from dissipation, according to others. It may have amounted to the same thing: Hastings had got the girl but had lost his life.[7]

GILES ST. AUBYN, one of Bertie's biographers, observed that it is precisely because nineteenth-century British society pretended to be so puritanical that getting caught breaking the rules was punished so severely.[8] Careers were ruined; homes were broken; blackmail flourished. Children born out of wedlock posed a particular threat, especially to European royal figures: a baby could grow up to claim the throne.

Bertie, with his numerous dalliances, was especially vulnerable; and, as he approached his middle years, frequently was in trouble. Not long before his thirtieth year, for example, he received a letter from an Italian named Pirro Benini, offering to sell the correspondence between Bertie and Benini's sister Giulia Barveci, who had just died. St. Aubyn describes Giulia as "one of the most breathtaking courtesans of the Second Empire who described herself as 'the greatest whore in the world.'"[9]

Benini proposed to sell the letters at public auction unless Bertie purchased them immediately. Conferences were held. Bertie's private secretary took charge. An Italian banker was consulted. An armed raid to recover the letters was considered. Negotiations were conducted. Eventually Bertie's representatives bought back the collection, which included letters from other prominent men.

Another potential scandal that threatened to erupt at the same time concerned an aristocratic lady named Lady Susan Vane Tempest, daughter of the fifth Duke of Newcastle. Lady Susan had a self-destructive taste in men, having insisted on marrying one who was mad, a drunkard, penniless, and subject to delirium tremens. When her husband died, she was consoled for a time by Bertie; but he soon made her pregnant, and she was afraid to tell him. When she finally did so, he apparently advised her to have an abortion. "*Too late* and *too* dangerous," she replied. Little is known of the rest of her life, except that she died—young—a short time later.

IN THE LATE 1870s, the structure of Bertie's love life in England changed.

Emilie Charlotte le Breton, a clergyman's daughter from the island of Jersey, had married a widower named Edward Langtry, from Belfast. She and her husband arrived in London at the beginning of 1877, knowing practically nobody; but word of her beauty soon spread through society. It reached the ears of fashionable painters, one of whom, John Millais, immediately executed a portrait of her with a lily in her hand, which proved to be a sensation at the Royal Academy. She wore no jewelry, appeared simple and artless, and was known as the Jersey Lily. In May 1877, four months after her unheralded arrival in London, the twenty-three-year-old clergyman's daughter from the Channel Islands found herself seated next to the Prince of Wales at a dinner party—at his request.[10] During her brief stay in London she had had liaisons with many of the highest in the land, but retained an air of innocence and seemed surprised at first that her husband was annoyed. (Later he accepted the situation with good grace.)

Soon the Prince of Wales was horseback riding with Lillie Langtry every morning. She became something like an official mistress, moved in society, and was even presented to the Queen—at Victoria's request. As was pointed out by John Pearson, a chronicler of Bertie's amours, Lillie provided an extramarital affair that was safe. She was respectable, and everything was out in the open. There were no scandals or blackmailing love letters or challenges to duels or children born out of wedlock—or so all concerned believed. But, after five years with Lillie as his mistress, Bertie broke with her when she *did* produce a child.

The Prince turned next to Sarah Bernhardt, the most glamorous actress of her age, or of any other. She was not his type—she was skinny and he liked them voluptuous—but she was a star, and he, a star himself, enjoyed consorting with the famous.

Daisy Brook, later Countess of Warfield, was another official mistress some years later. She reigned from 1891 to 1898.

Bertie lived his love life in different worlds. There were women he encountered on his travels; others whom he knew in French and British society; girls of the stage, and stars of all sorts; famous courtesans in France; and, also in France, his other homeland, the bordello life that became so glamorous and luxurious in the last two decades of the nineteenth century.

THE HOUSES OF PROSTITUTION for which France, in particular, was to become so famous—or infamous—were established at the start of the nineteenth century.

In 1802, at a time when Napoleon Bonaparte governed France as First Consul, the French state empowered municipalities to authorize the establishment of bordellos. It was to be done with the permission of the local police department. Houses were to be managed by women, not men. A regulatory scheme was put in motion to (among other things) prevent the spread of venereal disease. Its effect was to keep prostitution—as well as the crimes that often flourish around it—under the supervision of the police.

The object of this initiative was to bring the underworld out into the light and to sanitize it. Proponents of the legislation saw in it a way of defending the family by, in effect, incorporating what had been extramarital into the family scheme. Young men were taken to the brothel to be initiated: to acquire the necessary experience before marrying. Married men, in turn, subject to temptations that might otherwise endanger family life, could have their flings without thinking for a moment of leaving their wives. Houses developed to meet special needs. Thus in Paris two establishments catered to the tastes of priests, who were, of course, sworn to celibacy.[11]

It goes without saying that the life of the street continued to exist, outside the law, and with its own milieu of thieves, procurers, and murderers.

In 1878 the Chabanais—the first of the luxury bordellos—opened. It was at the start of the Third Republic, which proved to be, in terms of quality, the golden age of the legalized houses. Sumptuous meals were served; superb wines were available; and the women, geisha-style, offered conversation as well as sex.

The bordello was situated on the rue Chabanais, a tiny street near the Bourse and the Palais Royal. It runs for the length of a city block and is discreetly cut off by the rue des Petits Champs on one side and a small park on the other. A series of plaques remind us today that the street was opened by the Marquis de Chabanie in 1773; that Viollet-le-Duc, the nineteenth-century architectural restorer of Carcassonne, was among its residents; and that Stendhal, author of *The Red and the Black*, and Mérimée, the author of *Carmen*, used to meet with Viollet-le-Duc there.

Soon other luxury houses opened as well, notably the One Two Two at 122 rue de Provence, which later became a restaurant. A guidebook to the houses appeared in 1892. In seventy pages it listed establishments not only in Paris, but in several other European cities. Quantity was down; quality, up.

The rooms at the Chabanais became famous for their furnishings. Each had its character. One had Hindu paneling. The Japanese room, which in 1900 was entered into competition at the Exposition Universelle in Paris, was awarded first prize at the Exposition. A Moorish room, centered around a painting called *Le Viol*—The Rape—was much in demand; as was the Louis XVI room.

Bertie was encouraged by "the house" to furnish his own room at the Chabanais to meet his own requirements; and he did so. Bertie's room had a large bed—king-size we would say today, on all counts—with four columns draped in what appears to be gold. Its dimensions suited his own: there was ample room for him to move around. At the Chabanais, as in other houses that had rooms reserved for him, Bertie had sets of stirrups and saddles—silent witnesses of his need for help as he grew older.

The Prince also ordered an enormous bathtub with, as a "prow," the head of a woman; when it was filled with champagne, he would frolic in it with the prettiest of the resident young women. Later the tub passed into the hands of Salvador Dalí.

A famous piece that has come down to us was made to measure in

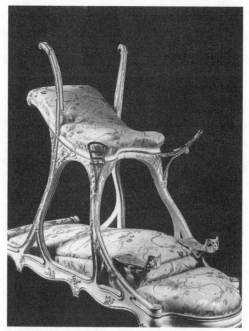

The fauteuil d'amour *created for Edward VII and housed in his room in the Parisian bordello Chabonais.*

1890 by the furniture maker Soubrier of Paris. It is a *fauteuil d'amour* ("chair of love"). According to the furniture expert Bruce M. Newman, in his authoritative *Fantasy Furniture* (1989), "it was made in the rococo style . . . and it was gilded and painted over wood."[12]

The Prince had become extremely stout. It no longer was feasible for him to lie on top; he might crush his partner. The *fauteuil d'amour* that he designed overcame such difficulties and afforded opportunities.

It was a kind of chaise longue that rested on the floor. Rising from it was a luxurious reclining chair in an ingenious design that suggested uses as a double bed. Golden stirrups protruding from the bottom level were positioned in such a way as to practically require one participant to lie on his or her back. Wheelbarrow-style arms enabled the Prince to leverage himself in thrusting. The games that could be played on this double-decker love machine were various and fantastic. The chaise was so designed that the Prince could have sexual relations with two women at the same time. Oddly enough, two-at-a-time also was a favorite pleasure of his chief adversary, Kaiser William II of Germany, though they were hardly likely to have confided as much to each other.

CLOSELY RELATED TO Bertie's love of France was a new love: Monte Carlo. Established in the 1860s, the casino and its surrounding luxuries and luxury hotels were the creation of a French financier, François Blanc. It catered almost entirely to what Victorian society regarded as vices. Monte Carlo became a regular stop on Bertie's European tours. He ate and drank and gambled. He dallied with the Grandes Horizontales—the French courtesans who were stars of their profession.

The three outstanding Horizontales of Belle Époque France were generally acknowledged to be La Belle Otero, Liane de Pougy, and—above all—Émilienne d'Alençon, known as "notre courtisane nationale."[13]

Mary Blume, historian of the Riviera, tells us that one of those famous ladies—La Belle Otero—with whom Bertie made love, won millions at the casino by betting on red twenty-one times in a row. In addition to Bertie, she bedded Czar Nicholas II of Russia, Leopold II of Belgium, Alfonso XIII of Spain, and Reza Shah; her body was so fetishized that "her exemplary breasts served as the model for the twin cupolas of the Carlton Hotel in Cannes . . ."[14]

The Grandes Horizontales were women for whom men had to pay immense fortunes; but they were sexually monogamous: they were kept by only one man at a time. Moreover, they allowed themselves to be kept only by men who pleased them.

IT WAS IN 1898, toward the twilight of his life as a womanizer, that Bertie met Alice Keppel. She was short, with fashionably small hands and feet, but was on her way to plumpness. He was, by then, immensely stout; and Alix's biographer tells us that "once when Queen Alexandra saw them together squeezed into a carriage she shook with laughter . . ."[15]

Alice and Bertie, almost immediately, became lovers. They were quite open about it. She went almost everywhere with him, much as though she were his wife. They stayed together for the rest of his life—some twelve years—even as impotence apparently took hold of him. She served as his official mistress, a *maîtresse en titre*: a Madame de Pompadour or du Barry. Taking such an established woman when a man reaches a certain age is a French sort of thing to do—and Bertie was very French.

Indeed in almost every respect, Bertie—forgetting for a moment how unusual were the opportunities that came his way—lived the life of a Third Republic Frenchman. To understand his outlook one has only to read the relevant pages in the first volume of Theodore Zeldin's magisterial *France 1848–1945*, entitled *Ambition, Love and Politics:* "Money played such a large part in marriage, sexual relations were subject to so many restrictions, wives were so keen to transform themselves from brides into matriarchs that inevitably adultery and prostitution were essential to the working of this system."

TRAVELING ABROAD provided Bertie with an apparently limitless supply of willing females; at home the same effect was produced by the house parties that, as the leader of society, he helped to make popular. British high society at the time, it has been estimated, consisted of about ten thousand people. In society, husbands were proud that their wives had a liaison with the Prince who was going to be a king. It was not just that hostesses made arrangements to facilitate his conquests: wives were invited to stay when their husbands were away, or were assigned a bedchamber on the far side of the house from their husbands.

There seems to be no doubt but that Bertie enjoyed these flirtations. We do not know how far they went. As he grew older, he was less able to sustain his earlier pace. There may have been caresses, fondlings, touches, and kisses rather than consummations; and for someone like Bertie, who seemed both to have loved women and to have loved romance, those might have been satisfying too.

Margot Asquith, witty wife of the Edwardian Prime Minister, remarked, "It would be wrong to assume that the King's only interest in women was to have an 'affaire' with them. That he had many 'affaires' is indisputable, but there were a great many other women in his life from whom all he sought was a diverting companionship."[16] A case in point was Agnes Keyser, a longtime friend with whom he shared interests. Agnes, together with her sister, founded a nursing home for officers during the Boer War; after the war this institution became the King Edward VII Hospital for Officers, which both she and Edward continued to support.

. . .

LIKE THEODORE ROOSEVELT, his future political partner, Edward was in part a self-invented character. The one was not entirely a playboy. The other was not entirely a frontiersman.

IN THE LAST DECADE of his life, Bertie lived the comfortable life of a prosperous Frenchman: one wife and one openly lived-with mistress. To the end he adored the company and the conversation of his female friends. He began by merely loving sex and ended by loving women.

THE INTERNATIONAL EXHIBITION of 1900 in Paris put on display eighty thousand exhibits spread out over 277 acres. The Eiffel Tower alone, built earlier, attracted a million visitors.

As France's fin-de-siècle party, the Exhibition literally celebrated the end of the nineteenth century. It would mark another event: Bertie's last year as Prince of Wales. But he was remembered. In France, someone like Bertie came to be called a Milord Anglais.

Even as a boy he had been fascinated by clothes. Now it was because of him that men had their trousers pressed at the sides rather than in front, and that they wore the hat known as a homburg. Men left the bottom of their jackets unbuttoned, and still do; though we do it to be fashionable and he did it to accommodate his paunch.

Apocryphal though it may be, the story persists that he invented at least one popular dessert. He was dining with a lovely young Frenchwoman (so runs the story) named Suzette, and at the end of the meal she ordered crêpes in a brandy sauce. The headwaiter leaned over to light a candle on the table; but dropped the match. Up in flames went the brandy sauce. With profuse apologies, the headwaiter started for the kitchen to order more crêpes. But Bertie, smelling the tempting odor of the flaming sauce, sampled the crêpes, pronounced them delicious, and decided always to order crêpes in a brandy sauce that was flaming. In honor of his lovely young companion, he dubbed his dessert creation Crêpes Suzette.

Can it really have been true?

AT SOME POINT during or after the 1914 war, the last decade of Bertie's tenure as Prince of Wales came to be especially associated with him. *La Belle Époque*, a vague phrase, evokes him; so does *fin de siècle*.

Above all the Belle Époque of the nineties and afterward was a time of joyousness—or at least was remembered as such. He was as much a regular of Paris nightlife as was the painter Henri de Toulouse-Lautrec. Spotted entering the Moulin Rouge one night, he was greeted familiarly by the dancer La Goulue: *"Ullo, Wales! Est-ce que tu vas payer mon champagne?"* [Hello, Wales! Are you going to pick up my champagne tab?] Answer: Yes.

The Folies-Bergère, a Parisian music hall and vaudeville house, had flourished for decades; but the striptease, introduced in 1894, soon overshadowed the various other shows and productions. It was a chief tourist attraction and, for many, epitomized France. Like the notorious Maxim's, a sort of clubhouse for the aristocracy, it stood for the kind of life supposedly lived by the Prince of Wales and his social set during the Belle Époque. It was the High Life, pronounced by the French "Le Hig Leef."

It was understandable that Bertie's contemporaries, who had watched his progress with some dismay, assumed that someone who had entirely given over his life to pleasure would not be prepared to deal with the manifold affairs of a global empire.

They were wrong.

11 BERTIE'S POLITICS

THE OFFICIAL BIOGRAPHER of Edward VII notes that during the four decades in which Bertie was an adult heir to the throne, "the Prince constantly met the leading political players when out in society and would question them 'without reserve on pending crises.'"[1] Moreover he took a lively interest in government appointments high and low, pushing his own candidates and developing a following of his own. This circle of associates was an additional supplier of current information.

Then, too, since 1863, he had been seated in the House of Lords. That could have kept him, to some extent, aware of parliamentary opinion and issues.

On his frequent travels, he visited members of his family and of governments abroad, learning much from them. Another resource was the diplomatic corps in London: he entertained ambassadors, who were generally well informed. His parties were popular and well attended; anyone who mattered socially or politically would come. His education came from questioning the leading minds of the day.

An advantage of self-education of this sort was that it was au-
thentic: Bertie actually dealt with political figures in person. It was
not book-learning or even newspaper-learning; his information came
directly from the primary sources. He did not have to read about
Garibaldi; he knew him. Here was the very opposite of the education
that Prince Consort Albert had tried to give him. His was education
on the ground. As politics is in significant part an effort to form cor-
rect judgments about other people, Bertie's experience in dealing
over the years with the key individuals in the important European
governments, and in observing them, gave him valuable insight into
what was going on.

The sheer length of time during which he was outside looking in
proved an advantage. The thirty or forty years during which, with
respect to issues that interested him, he questioned leaders on all sides
of controversies—and then watched to see what in fact came about,
and who was right and who was wrong, and sometimes even why—
turned him into a kind of walking history of the last half of the
nineteenth century.

Many historians, perhaps even most, deprecate his abilities; and
political leaders such as Arthur Balfour, who claimed credit for his
accomplishments, tried to belittle them, and him, after his death. But
when it came to Europe's international politics in his time, it only
slightly exaggerates to say that he had known everyone and been
everywhere. By way of contrast, his most famous Foreign Secretary,
Sir Edward Grey, took office, in the mid-1900s, without having ever
set foot outside the British Isles.

Around 1897, while he still was Prince of Wales, Bertie became
acquainted with someone his own age who proved to be particularly
useful. He was Sir Donald Mackenzie Wallace, Director of the Foreign Department—which is to say, foreign editor—of the *Times* of

London. Well traveled and well informed, Wallace sent confidential reports to Bertie, keeping him up-to-date. Wallace was especially expert on Russia and Eastern Europe.

In 1902–1903, after Bertie became King, Wallace went on to become editor of the new edition of the *Encyclopaedia Britannica*. But he continued to belong to the inner group of the monarch's messengers and advisers who were able to keep Bertie informed on European and world affairs.

PART THREE

WILLY CASTS
A SHADOW

12 | WILLY BITES

IT WAS A SOURCE of relief in Prussia—of relief, but also of joy—that Vicki had become pregnant. It was 1858. The King was childless. He also was legally incompetent; so his sixty-two-year-old brother, Fritz's father, served as Regent in his stead.

When Vicki's baby was born on January 27, 1859, and was a boy, the dynasty of the Hohenzollerns was secured. There now was a clear line of male succession. The throne would pass from Fritz's uncle to Fritz's father to Fritz to Fritz's newborn son. The baby was the first heir born to the Hohenzollerns in twenty-one years.

A medical team including specialists had attended the mother, and, mother to daughter, Victoria had sent her own personal physician. Due to the peculiar prudery prevalent at the time, when doctors treated royal females, the physicians were obliged to operate under the woman's skirts—literally at arm's length. The medical team's terrible finding was that the baby was in breech position. At the time, only 2 percent of breech babies were born alive. The finding came too late to do much about it. The only gynecologist on the team, a

Dr. Edouard Arnold Martin, performed miracles in maneuvering the baby. It was a close call; after appearing to be dead, the child was delivered alive. But he bore forever the mark of the forceps that had dragged him into the world: a withered arm.

The baby was named William. The family called him Willy. His birth had been a painful one, as had Bertie's. While Victoria resented her son, a difficult birth seems to have helped make Willy hate his mother.

Willy had been badly injured, emotionally as well as physically. The paralyzed left arm was visible, giving Willy an unbalanced look, but he was unbalanced emotionally too. Professor C. G. Röhl, author of the in-progress definitive biography of the Kaiser, has studied in detail the personality disorders that can result from the particular experiences that Willy underwent. Among other things, Röhl tells us that the oxygen supply to the baby's brain may have been affected.

Did he suffer brain damage? Nobody knows for sure. But certainly he must have reacted in some way to the barbaric medical treatments the doctors inflicted upon him as he was growing up in an effort to cure his arm—one of which was to place him in a "head-stretching machine."

IN CLASSICAL ATHENS, some twenty-five centuries ago, Euripides, considered to be the most tragic of the Greek playwrights, presented a deceptive and relevant new play, called *Alexander*. In it, Hecuba, Queen of Troy, dreams that she is about to give birth to a firebrand. Terrified, she orders some cattlemen in her employ to kill the infant. Instead, they save it and bring it up among themselves as one of their own. Years later Hecuba repents. She initiates funeral games in honor of her supposedly slain son. The games are won by her son, who believes himself to be just one of the cattlemen. But he is recognized. Amidst rejoicing he comes into his own. He takes his rightful place as Paris, Prince of Troy.

This was a familiar story, common to many cultures: the newborn child who is to be abandoned or killed, but instead is saved by people who bring him up as one of their own, and then, when grown to manhood, is recognized and occupies his rightful position. It is a simple and romantic tale, apparently with a happy ending, which leaves the audience cheerful. But that is not the way that Euripides tells it. For his audience would have known that Paris did indeed bring ruin and death. He *was* the firebrand. The terrible prophecy of doom was to come true. He did bring destruction to his city. The Trojans celebrating the restoration of their young prince in fact were applauding their own impending death and the total destruction of their city.

Something of that sort was occurring in Germany in 1859. Prussians fired off a one-hundred-gun salute to the newborn child, and joyous messages poured in; but Willy was to prove a calamitous ruler who would contribute importantly to many of the tragedies of his time. Of course, they could not know it at the time, but Germans, like Euripides' Trojans, were celebrating their own coming ruin.

WHEN THE YOUNG PRINCE William was one year old, he displayed alarming signs of violence. His mother no longer dared take him on her lap; he scratched her neck and face and (she wrote) "is getting very wild and unmanageable."

At the age of four, Willy was allowed to cross the Channel to attend the marriage of his young uncle Bertie to the lovely Danish Princess Alix. He was a nuisance, throwing things and generally behaving badly. Two dukes scolded the young boy. He responded by biting their legs. This could have been considered a portent of things to come, but, at the time, was not. Indeed his mother reported that he was a "darling little creature . . . perfectly behaved . . . very funny & good-natured,"[1] although in another mood said "the idea of his remaining a cripple haunts me."[2]

It was only gradually, over the course of a half century, and during times of stress and crisis, that some of those who dealt with him came to believe that he was not quite normal; but the evidence, even today, is not conclusive. Much of it comes from people who had a score to settle with him. It is only in our own time that scholars, above all C. G. Röhl, have studied in detail the effect on the Kaiser of his traumatic childbirth. Röhl quotes his doctors (when Willy was about thirty years old) as warning that he "was not, and never would be, a normal man," that when angry he often would be "quite incapable of forming a reasonable or temperate judgment"; and that, though he probably would not become clinically insane, "some of his actions would probably be those of a man not wholly sane."[3] According to Röhl, they warned that his mounting the throne could be "a danger to Europe."[4]

The British Prime Minister, Lord Salisbury, who in 1887–1888 had information about Willy's mental health, worried that he "was not quite normal."[5] The French foreign ministry in 1892 reported that he was "mentally ill." The Austro-Hungarian Military Attaché in Berlin claimed that he was "not quite sane" and had "as one says, a screw loose."[6]

In recent times, scholars have explained other aspects of his personality and behavior as a repressed homosexuality, of which, however, he seems to have been unaware. His best friend, Philipp zu Eulenburg, eventually was exiled for his role in a homosexual scandal that reached the law courts; but in the 1890s Eulenburg's cabal influenced policymaking and official appointments in Berlin. It is not clear whether, at that time, the Kaiser was aware of his friend's proclivities.

Röhl tells us that "the Kaiser loved uniforms, historical costumes, jewellery and games, most of all childish pranks in all-male company."[7] These were tastes he continued to indulge. His chosen companions competed in creating stunts to amuse him. Two of them pretended to be Siamese twins by tying themselves together with a large sausage. A future German Foreign Minister persuaded a colleague, "You must be paraded by me as a circus poodle!—That will be a 'hit' like nothing else.... Just think how wonderful when you bark, howl to music, shoot off a pistol or do other tricks. It is simply *splendid*!" Röhl tells us that in 1908, a member of the Kaiser's military inner circle died when dancing for the Emperor in a large feather hat and a tutu.[8]

Despite Willy's preference for male companionship, he was actively heterosexual both before and after his marriage. Historical detective work has shown that he had a taste for two women at a time, and that he had a fetish for beautiful hands.

From the outset, the half-German side of him was at war with the half-English side. He was wildly jealous of the British, wanting to be British, wanting to be better at being British than the British were, while at the same time hating them and resenting them because he never could be fully accepted by them.

He hated his mother, possibly because he blamed her for his botched birth, or perhaps because he suspected—quite unjustly—that, because he was a cripple, she did not love him and was not proud of him. But she too was a difficult person, and may have expressed lavish affection (according to Röhl) only because it was expected of

her. Many of the outsize personalities of the era were odd or harbored strange tastes; the Victorian age was full of them, and in this
Willy was not alone.

WILLY'S PARENTS did not have the last word in regard to his upbringing. His grandfather—Germany's ruler—was supreme in this
respect as in so many others. Even Willy's tutor was selected by William I and was employed by him.

What made life especially difficult for Willy's parents, Fritz and
Vicki, was that their faction at the Prussian court was in the process
of losing out in the 1860s. Their circle was pro-English, constitution-
alist, and broadly liberal. William I had come over almost completely
to the side of their adversaries, the reactionary, pro-Russian clique.
Where politics were concerned, Willy's father and Willy's grandfather were barely on speaking terms. As will be seen, Willy in his
adolescent years was to take advantage of this situation.

How Willy, who one day would be king, was to be educated and
by whom, was destined to be a subject of intense controversy. Parents
and grandparents fought over it, with Willy's mother emerging as the
essential winner. The two positions to be filled were those of civilian
and military tutor. Georg Hinzpeter—not Vicki's first choice, but a
fallback—was chosen for the civilian post, and held it until Willy was
eighteen. As Willy's biographer Christopher Clark tells us, the young
Prince's studies with Hinzpeter began at six in the morning and lasted
until six or seven in the evening, six days a week. He studied "Latin,
history, religion, mathematics, and modern languages."[9] In this, as in
so many things, Willy was unlike his British uncle: the punishing
academic schedule—twelve hours a day, six days a week—that Ber-

tie had found intolerable was accepted by Willy, seemingly without any problem. His program included "visits to mines, workshops, factories and homes of the laboring poor."[10]

Willy's military tutor resigned when he realized that civilian studies would take up the major share of Willy's time. In the ensuing disputes, in which the King took part, Vicki wrote to her mother, "I think this interference in our concerns too bad. You have no idea what trouble the reigning party takes to put their spies about our court, nor to what degree they hate us."[11]

Vicki won her war. She succeeded in sending her son to a civilian school—a *gymnasium* with children his own age; and then on to university in Bonn. His military schooling was relatively slight; Christopher Clark calls him a "military dilettante."[12]

As Willy entered adolescence, like teenagers elsewhere, he yearned for independence. For many, perhaps for most, thirteen, fourteen, and fifteen are the difficult ages. Already resentful of his mother, he rebelled against his parents by siding with the one person who could free him: his grandfather, the King. It was the King who made the rules and who paid the bills.

By adopting the politics of William I, and of William's all-powerful minister, Count Otto von Bismarck, Willy moved out from under the control of his parents, starting at the age of fifteen. Whether he was consciously adopting a policy, or whether he fell into it unthinkingly, he ended by joining the party of government against the powerless party of opposition.

Willy was growing into puberty during the exciting decade in which Prussia won mastery of the German-speaking world. It was

Bismarck's triumph, empowered by Willie's grandfather, William I; and it was achieved on the battlefield by Count Helmuth von Moltke, Chief of the General Staff.

Germany's triumph under Bismarck's leadership began with the obscure but vexing Schleswig-Holstein dispute between Denmark and Prussia, which had so distressed Bertie and Alix. In 1864, Prussia, allying with Austria, fought Denmark and won Schleswig-Holstein. Two years later, in 1866, Prussia attacked Austria, defeating it, taking nothing from it, but excluding it, from then on, from "Germany." In 1870–1871, Prussia provoked France into a war; won it; annexed French territories on the frontier, Alsace and parts of Lorraine; and brought together most of the German states (except Austria) in a federation under the King of Prussia, who thereupon became Emperor ("Kaiser") of Germany.

At the time, and from then on, it was said that Bismarck had unified Germany. His achievement was great, but perhaps it was not *that* achievement. A British historian, L. C. B. Seaman, pointed out long ago, "It was *a* German Empire, certainly, but it was not, and Bismarck never intended it to be, *the* German Empire. It excluded, deliberately, all the Germans living within the Hapsburg territories of Austria and Bohemia. Thus Bismarck's German Empire was based on the division of Germany, not its unification."[13]

Bismarck had split the German-speaking world into two: one predominantly Protestant empire and one predominantly Catholic empire. For Protestant Prussian nationalists that was not merely enough, it was more than enough. Bismarck's new federal structure was, however, a fragile one. It consisted of four kingdoms, six grand duchies, three free cities, and the imperial provinces of Alsace and parts of Lorraine. Its engine was the kingdom of Prussia. Its focal point was the army, which united under the leadership of the Prussian King in time of war.

It was a heady time to be alive for a German nationalist, especially one destined by birth to play a great role in the country's future, and impatient to start receiving credit for doing great things.

In 1881 Willy married. His bride was Augusta Victoria, Princess of Schleswig-Holstein-Sonderburg-Augustenburg ("Dona"). She was largely Vicki's choice, yet turned out to be anti-English, illiberal, and dull. Poor Vicki! Her nominees rarely were chosen; and when they were they turned out to have been of the enemy camp.

Like his uncle Bertie, Willy took his marriage as a rite of passage, entitling him to greater independence. It was in the decade that followed, the 1880s, that he developed and matured; in these years he also apprenticed in politics.

Christopher Clark, one of Willy's recent biographers, has reminded readers of an important aspect of the future Kaiser's apprenticeship. It is usual for the dauphin to live in the shadow of his powerful father, the king. But in Willy's case, his father was powerless; it was his grandfather who was powerful. Moreover his father and grandfather were on opposite sides. His father was a constitutional liberal in the English and Saxe-Coburg traditions, while his grandfather was guided by Bismarck, the reactionary Prussian, who served as Chancellor of the Germany that he had created: Bismarck, the man with the dueling scars; Bismarck, the man of blood and iron.

BISMARCK, AND HIS SON and junior partner, Herbert, took steps to reward Willy for moving into the political orbit of William I. They sent the young prince on a mission to czarist Russia.

Willy, when in Russia, and by letters to Russia after his return, launched into discussions of European high diplomacy, repeating details of confidential conversations in which he had participated, and claiming that his father, Fritz, had denounced the Czar: "there was no hateful adjective which he did not use to paint you in the darkest of hues..."[14] Denouncing England and his mother and father, Willy pledged himself, once he came to power, to support Russia and the Czar.

Willy came away from his trip to Russia determined—when one day his time came—to rule as the Czar ruled. He would be an absolute monarch: an autocrat.

Willy worshipped success, and was drawn to men of great power or great wealth. Growing up in a family split by politics, polarized, but with the decisions finally and always made by the King, the grandfather, not by the Crown Prince, his father, the youthful Willy joined the winners. He sided with his grandfather against his father. For other reasons he was against his mother, and unforgivingly so. The approval that men usually seek from their mothers was sought by Willy from his grandmother, the greatest crowned head of his time, the Queen of England.

As it happened, each of these two reigning monarchs, Victoria and William I, ruled for a very long time. The British Queen, who later became Queen-Empress, ruled from 1837 to 1901. The Prussian King, who later became German Emperor, ruled from 1861 to 1888. So Willy, and even more so Bertie, served a long apprenticeship in which tutelage was essentially political. Battles were fought to shape them and to win their allegiance. The story of Bertie's education was more simply told. But neither young prince emerged in his twenties as their mentors had intended.

. . .

ONLY NOW, with the enormous and revealing work in the archives by C. G. Röhl, can the full irony of Willy's upbringing be appreciated. Röhl writes that "As a counterweight to the often astonishingly progressive and at all events decidedly Anglophile principles which . . ." Willy's parents "entertained, Kaiser William I, the military party at the Prussian Court and the Bismarck family all endeavored to influence the education and political outlook of the physically handicapped young Prince, to mould into a Prussian—reactionary, masculine—militaristic and anti-Semitic bastion against the enlightened goals of his parents, which they abhorred as 'soft,' 'feminine,' and 'un-German.' Aghast, the Crown Prince and Crown Princess were forced to realize that at the age of twenty-one their son and heir had already turned his back on them and their cause." But before long he turned his back on the other side too. "Not until it was too late did the Bismarcks and their advisers realize that the impulsive, cold, egotistical young Hohenzollern Prince, with his thirst for power and glory, posed a danger not only to themselves, but also to the German Reich and the peace of Europe. 'Woe unto my poor grandchildren!' sighed Bismarck . . . as Willy mounted the throne as Kaiser William."[15]

WILLY'S GRANDFATHER, Kaiser William I, did not die until the age of ninety. Willy's father then briefly ascended the throne as Kaiser Frederick III. Already the new monarch—Fritz, Willy's father—was in the grip of an advanced cancer; and the brevity of his reign proved to be a disaster for Germany and for Europe. He was not given a chance to try to realize the Victoria and Albert dream of a liberal and constitutional Continent. He was not even able to begin along that road. It was apparent from the start that Frederick's regime would be only temporary. When he was crowned, his wife Vicki, the new Empress, wrote to her mother, Queen Victoria: "I think people in general consider us a mere passing shadow, soon to be replaced by reality in the shape of William."[16]

IN THE POLITICAL world in which Willy grew to young manhood—in the 1880s, in other words, when he was in his twenties—Great Britain, although it still was the leading power, found itself isolated. It happened because the other Great Powers of Europe wanted to expand at the same time, in some cases threatening England's possessions. Even Germany, which hitherto had restrained itself under Bismarck's leadership, suddenly turned around and carved out for itself a large colonial empire in Africa. Thus the other European countries became England's rivals simultaneously.

The United Kingdom, meanwhile, failed to set priorities for itself. Should it defer to Germany in Africa in return for German friendship in Europe? Should it make concessions to France in North Africa in order to solicit French support elsewhere? Briefly, which should come first for England: Europe or the overseas empire?

When Willy was in his twenties, the British faced danger on almost all sides. In the 1880s British-led armies were defeated, and indeed wiped out, by local armies in the Sudan. France continued to contest England's presence in Egypt. Russia, advancing on Afghanistan in the so-called Penjdeh crisis of 1885, was seen by London as a threat to India.

Willy, who continued his communications with the Russian court, supplied St. Petersburg with information and with incitements to take a hard line against the Britons. He cheered on the Sudanese, and encouraged the Russians to make war.

When it came to foreign policy, the English administration of Liberal Prime Minister William Gladstone had proved to be a disaster. The Conservative leader, the third Marquess of Salisbury, taking office in 1885, brought Great Britain back from the brink. The war clouds blew away. Willy's hopes were disappointed.

In this case, "people in general"—those who had regarded Frederick's reign as a mere passing shadow—proved to be right. Frederick III served as Emperor of Germany for a mere ninety-nine days. He had no time to start anything; as it turned out, it was as though he had just been a voyager passing through. He died June 15, 1888.

Willy now ascended the throne as William II. He came to it with scores to settle—above all, with his mother. He claimed that she had treated him "like a dog."[17] Willy had been in the habit of giving out photographs of himself carrying the motto: "I bide my time."[18] Now his time had come. His time was June 15, 1888.

ON THE DAY OF HIS coronation Willy summoned the commander of the guard of the castle in which his father lay dying. He issued new orders. "The moment you receive the message that the Kaiser is dead," Willy commanded, occupy the castle "and let no one out, without exception."[19]

At a blow, he had made his mother his prisoner: from the guarded castle, surrounded by hussars, there was no escape. But the treasure he sought had eluded him. Starting the year before, and until just before Fritz's death, Vicki had been forwarding trunks filled with Fritz's diaries and other important papers to the safety of London.

Six such trunks in all now reposed in the custody of Queen Victoria. The last of the six trunks had gone out just before Fritz died, through the good offices of the British Ambassador in Berlin, who was given to understand that it contained Vicki's jewelry.

But Willy had placed his mother—the mother he hated so much—under what amounted to house arrest. Eventually Vicki retired from public life. She retreated to her home in the Taunus mountains, where she was allowed to live.

13 | WILLY BARKS

CROWNED KING AND EMPEROR, ruler of Prussia and leader of federal Germany, Willy was transformed into Kaiser William II. He always had displayed an unjustifiably high opinion of his own intellect and of his military prowess. Now he surrounded himself with sycophants who fed his arrogance and his vanity. Formerly he had schemed and lied to get his way; now he gave orders. His political ideas—if they can be called ideas—were not even old-fashioned: they were feudal. He believed in the divine right of kings; and in private communications even said so.

He confused countries with their monarchs; and because he also was given to violent mood swings, his foreign policy could be dizzyingly inconsistent. As a young man he had looked up to the Archduke Rudolf, heir to the Hapsburg Empire, a hunting and wenching companion; but he quickly shifted views and looked down upon him. In tandem were his views of Austria-Hungary: up one day, down the next.

Other than his hatred of his mother, the one constant in his political and personal constellation of tangled views was his passionate dislike of his uncle Bertie. Shortly after William became Kaiser, he demanded that the Prince of Wales leave Vienna—which the Prince then was visiting—and remain away, as long as he, the Kaiser, was in residence in the Hapsburg capital. When the episode blew up into a scandal, William simply denied it: he lied. A few years earlier, on a previous trip to Hapsburg lands in 1885, Willy had reported to his grandfather, the then Kaiser William I, that Bertie, supposedly staying there incognito, "had the stupidity to be seen in broad daylight . . . coming out of one of the most infamous Viennese brothels before walking about in the street!"[1]

William frequently took a dim view of the sex lives of his royal colleagues. What does it matter, he asked, if the King of Spain is overthrown? "Why does he run after the women?" Of what use was the heir to the throne of Romania? "He cannot do more than f——"

It might be thought that Willy's lifelong detestation of Bertie was due to the latter's freewheeling sex life; for Willy did censure others for their pursuit of illicit pleasures, especially, in the case of married men, after the marriage. But in that respect the young German monarch was no better than anyone else. William talked as though he were "pure"; and earlier biographers have respected that claim. But the indefatigable C. G. Röhl has uncovered evidence of one sexual adventure after another.

In Alsace in 1879, Willy entered into a relationship, possibly his first, with Emilie Klopp, who called herself "Miss Love." They had a child. Incriminating letters—love letters—much later were offered for sale; Willy lied about them, but was protected by the Bismarck family, which purchased the letters and similar ones from other women.

In the 1880s letters and other documents show a pattern of using call girls. A woman recommends a girlfriend for a meeting—Willy and the two of them. There are missed appointments and a final disagreement about Willy paying travel expenses. He asks for another engagement; they meet and take a single room for the night at an inn; the other guests complain of the noise they make. The lady remains, on a sporadic basis, part of his life: her name recurs.

Another lady regrets that she cannot come to him in Berlin at the end of August, as he asks, because she has a prior appointment in Switzerland; what about someday in the autumn?

At about this time Willy contacted Frau Wolf. Röhl tells us that she was "a famous Viennese procuress," who supplied him with lady companions. His expenses in this respect must have been considerable; he was driven to borrow large sums from Archduke Rudolf.[2]

FROM HIS GRANDFATHER, William I, Willy inherited the apparently all-powerful Chancellor Otto von Bismarck. The question, when Willy became William II, was who would rule. Before dying, William I confided to one of his intimates that "when Prince Wilhelm is Kaiser he will insist on appearing as the man who really rules—that is why I do not think he and the chancellor will agree for long."[3]

That turned out to be true. It explains a great deal about Wilhelmine Germany. It explains why the new Kaiser always surrounded himself with flatterers and yes-men. But it also explains why several of the most disastrous decisions of his reign were ones in which he allowed himself to be overruled by his government: if it looked as though a certain decision had to be made, he preferred that it appear to have been made on his authority. He wanted to seem to be the person in charge: to seem, but not necessarily to be.

In March 1890 Kaiser William II dismissed Chancellor von Bismarck. At that point there were many things that separated the two men, of which one was highly visible: Willy was in his twenties, while Bismarck was in his seventies. There were two closely related issues too: who should rule, and who should appear to rule.

Willy was vain. He loved to strut. He was theatrical. He was a scene-stealer; and so was Bismarck. There was no question but that the aging Chancellor would have to go.

At almost the same time that Bismarck was being dismissed, a decision had to be made that was perhaps the most fateful of Willy's reign: whether or not to renew the Reinsurance Treaty with Russia.

The only Great Power in Europe that bore a grudge against Germany was France. France had lost frontier territories, the province of Alsace and parts of Lorraine, to Bismarck's Germany in their 1870–1871 war. The French people passionately wanted to get these lands back. But France, after 1871, was not strong enough to take them. France would need the help of a powerful ally. So it had been Bismarck's policy to keep France isolated: to keep it, in other words, from finding such an ally.[4]

German-speaking Austria enjoyed a special relationship with Germany that included a secret treaty of alliance. In the secret Reinsurance Treaty, Germany promised to protect Russia against an Austrian attack (while Russia promised to side with Germany against a French attack).

For almost a century, Prussian-led Germany, Austria, and Russia had formed an ideological block in world affairs: a reactionary block dedicated to a defense of the divine right of kings. It might seem that when Bismarck drew the three empires closer together, he was doing no more than advancing their divinely inspired faith.

But Austria and Russia both aimed at expansion in the Balkans. That was where each of them envisioned their future growth. Austria saw it as Teutons conquering Slavs, while Russia saw it as Slavs liberating Slavs. Bismarck may well have seen his treaty relationships with his two allies as a policy of joining them in order to restrain them: in other words, as a way to keep the peace between them.

As Bismarck was being dismissed, the Russian ambassador in Berlin raised with the Kaiser (as Willy had become) the issue of renewing the Reinsurance Treaty before it lapsed: the Kaiser promised to renew it. But an anti-Bismarck faction in the German Foreign Office intercepted it. Among the leading figures in the German government who lobbied against it was Hans Lothar von Schweinitz, the ambassador to St. Petersburg, who was regarded as Berlin's expert on Russian affairs. He argued that secretly protecting one ally against the other was contradictory and therefore dishonorable. William was persuaded; he remarked that "if Schweinitz is also against it, then it cannot be done. I am extremely sorry, but I desire more than anything to pursue an honorable policy."[5]

As the world learned years later, the Reinsurance Treaty lapsed when the German government failed to renew it; and a rejected Russian government eventually accepted the only alliance on offer: with France. The French-Russian alliance from 1895 on became the central danger to Germany's world position. With French capital financing Russian railroads and armaments after the turn of the century, and, with Russia opening up a prospective second front in a future war, frightening possibilities appeared for the German military, haunted by the "encirclement" that—it is widely believed—their own government brought upon them by allowing the Reinsurance Treaty to lapse. German generals began to think in terms of launching a preventive first strike in a war that, as time went on, they more and more thought would be inevitable.

THE KAISER WAS AN embarrassment to Germany's military and civilian leaders. He was always changing his mind; and he was inconsistent. These were traits that, in large part, would only become visible once he had total power. As Christopher Clark tells us, "Wilhelm rarely formed hard-and-fast commitments. He could be roused to enthusiasm for any or all available policy options, including ones that had already been ruled out . . ."[6] He did not seem to understand the significance of policies that already had been adopted.

As he loved making striking and dramatic pronouncements, his staff would receive bold orders from him that he would have to rescind the next day. Sometimes without consulting anyone, he would issue statements that later would have to be explained away. At times he sounded or acted like an intelligent, well-informed man; while at other times he acted or sounded like a foolish one.

Often there was little follow-through on what he said or what he ordered. His bark was worse than his bite.

14 | WILLY SENDS A TELEGRAM

THE 1890S. EUROPEAN imperialism was in full bloom. The countries of Asia were at stake. So was Africa, at first for its shoreline needed by ships headed to the Orient, but later coveted for its own sake.

Over the years—indeed, over the centuries—the Europeans had established depots and coaling stations along the African route to the East, as well as agricultural colonies and markets to which migrant shepherds brought flocks. The populations were largely Dutch and German, although the Napoleonic Wars brought a British presence and an undefined English suzerainty of part of the European territories. The local Boers ("farmers") coexisted uneasily with the British and with the native black Africans; but such balance as existed was overthrown when rich deposits of gold and diamonds were discovered toward the end of the nineteenth century.

Britain found it especially unsettling that (in 1884) Germany carved out for itself an enormous territory in southwest Africa immediately above the English-governed Cape Colony.

. . .

IT WAS AT A TIME when imperialism was in the air. The industrialization of Europe at high speed led politicians to believe that their countries must acquire new territories and new markets. The creation of new countries in Europe itself—as Germany and Italy achieved nationhood—brought into the Great Powers new competitors that believed in their need to catch up in the quest for colonies. Modern science had conquered the deadly diseases like malaria that hitherto had protected Africa from invasion, while the invention of gunboats enabled the aggressive empires of Europe to project their power inland: penetrating the interior of the African continent through its river system. The European powers were locked in the biggest, fastest arms race in history. The single largest company in Europe was Krupp, an armaments manufacturer; and other giant arms manufacturers were not far behind.

A central date in the intellectual life of the imperialist age was 1886, when a then-obscure American naval officer, Alfred Thayer Mahan, delivered a series of lectures at the American Naval War College at Newport, Rhode Island. From the lectures emerged a book called *The Influence of Sea Power upon History*. When it was published in 1890, young Theodore Roosevelt reviewed it enthusiastically in the *Atlantic Monthly*. It was read, and indeed devoured, everywhere; it took the world by storm; it influenced people everywhere, even those who otherwise had little in common with one another. Among those deeply influenced was the German emperor, Kaiser William II. Germany's race to equal England's fleet seemed—at least to Britons—to serve no purpose unless it be war. But Bernhard von Bülow, speaking for Germany, said that it was to protect commerce and to win overseas colonies.

Philipp zu Eulenberg, who enjoyed the reputation of being the Kaiser's best friend, had succeeded in installing his candidate, Bülow, as Chancellor of Germany, a position analogous to that of prime minister. Working with Alfred von Tirpitz, Germany's naval head, Bülow began to pursue a Mahan-esque program at the turn of the century. Until then, Prussia, and the country it had unified, contented itself with being a land power: indeed the supreme one. "Now in 1900," as Winston Churchill later wrote (referring to Berlin's official naval policy), "came a Fleet Law of a very different kind."[1] Germany's official policy now included this proclamation: "In order to protect German trade and commerce under existing conditions only one thing will suffice, namely, Germany must possess a battle fleet of such strength that, even for the most powerful naval adversary, a war would involve such risks as to make the Power's own supremacy doubtful."

Englishmen took the German naval threat seriously. But Berlin denied that what it was doing was threatening. Years later, after the Great War of 1914–1918 was fought and lost, German Chancellor von Bülow wrote that his (and the Kaiser's) naval program was not intended to be warlike.

> Never, since we began to build our fleet, had William II seriously considered that he might have to use it in a war. He had only felt that a strong German navy was our safest rampart against peace-breakers—that the fleet could also, now and then, be the pretext for magnificent maneuvers. And that was all! On each he had his own luxurious staterooms, fitted out with special toilet apparatus. . . . His heart sank at the thought of having to sacrifice even one of these toys . . .[2]

A danger had arisen. Violence was in the air. The lure of empire dazzled and blinded. Kaiser William wanted to equal—or even exceed—the British.

THE ENGLISH DID NOT have to learn the lessons of naval power from Mahan; he had learned from them. From Tudor days onward, they had practiced forward defense, engaging the enemy not on their own shore but at sea or on the Continent. Ships were so much more rapid than land transport that they enjoyed all the advantages of mobility: they could hit here and there and everywhere.

Empire was something that had happened to England over the course of centuries; it was only in the lifetime of the Prince of Wales that it had become something more like a conscious ideology. When Queen Victoria added to her titles that of Empress of India, it was her own whim; it was not something asked for by her subjects.

It may have been the imperialists who were responsible for introducing a strain of violence into turn-of-the-century politics. Such was the opinion of Winston Churchill, writing several decades later: "I date the beginning of these violent times . . . from the Jameson Raid in 1896."[3] The Jameson Raid was an attempt by English South Africaners to take over the Boer country. It was mounted by disciples of the financier Cecil Rhodes and was inspired by the powerful Colonial Secretary Joseph Chamberlain. It failed; and Germans were conspicuously gleeful. Kaiser William and his aides sent President Paul Kruger, the Boer leader, a telegram of support on January 3, 1896. The message read as follows:

> I express to you my sincere congratulations that you and
> your people, without appealing to the help of friendly

powers, have succeeded, by your own energetic action against the armed bands which invaded your country as disturbers of the peace, in restoring peace and maintaining the independence of the country against attacks from without.

For once Germany cheered its emperor; and Britain, not for the first time, raged at him. The Prince of Wales was furious. Rarely can a short telegram have so electrified the political world. It alerted Britons; it was a signal that the outside world was hostile.

The Raid proved to be the precursor of the Boer War (1899–1902), in which Great Britain defeated South Africa despite the effective guerrilla warfare waged against it by the Boers. There was widespread sympathy for the Boer cause in Europe and even within Great Britain. The unpopularity of the war, combined with dismay at the initial losses in the fighting, caused Britain to reassess its position in the world. England had been far and away the greatest of powers. With its navy supreme in all the world's oceans, it knew no equal. Suddenly a guerrilla uprising had humbled it; the largest empire history had ever known had experienced intimations of mortality. Isolation, which had been a strength, now indicated vulnerability. All of Europe, or at least most, was aligning against the United Kingdom in support of the Boers. A new century called perhaps for alliances—and eventually for a retreat from empire.

ACROSS THE ATLANTIC Ocean, the United States moved in a pattern curiously parallel to that of the United Kingdom. In the mid-1890s, the time of the Jameson Raid, America too turned first assertive, and then expansive. At issue were Venezuela's frontiers with British Guiana, where gold recently had been discovered, as in South Africa. Taking up Venezuela's case, Secretary of State Richard Olney claimed, "To-day the United States is practically sovereign on this continent, and its fiat is law upon the subjects to which it confines its interposition."[4] President Grover Cleveland asserted Washington's rights under the Monroe Doctrine. British Prime Minister Lord Salisbury denied the validity of the Monroe Doctrine. In language that was much more cautious than at first appeared, the United States (through President Cleveland) seemed to be threatening war. Charles Campbell, a historian of these events, writes that "for a dreadful moment war seemed imminent"[5]—a war between England and America! That was in 1895. But "even at its height the war scare was limited in scope and intensity."[6] And 1895 was succeeded by 1896, a more amicable year, and in 1897 by a new American administration.

The Jameson Raid overshadowed the bickerings between Britons and Americans. Opinion in both countries swung toward a closer friendship—and in favor of settling disputes between them by arbitration rather than by warfare.

There were exceptions, however. The young politician Theodore Roosevelt wrote to his political patron and intimate friend Henry Cabot Lodge: "I do hope that there will not be any backdown among our people." He added, "I don't care whether our sea coast cities are bombarded or not; we would take Canada."[7]

15 WILLY CHALLENGES BERTIE

THE EUROPE IN WHICH Willy now played a leading role was dominated by six countries. These ranked as the Great Powers. They were Britain, Germany, Russia, France, Austria-Hungary, and (to some extent) Italy. Despite their formal status, the six were not equally powerful. To maintain or to increase their power relative to one another was the object of their foreign policies, and of the alliances among them by the terms of which they agreed to oppose or support one another. It also was the object of the arms race in which they were engaged: the greatest arms race the world had yet seen, which culminated in the Great War in 1914.

Apart from France, the Great Powers of the 1880s and 1890s were monarchies. To some extent, therefore—and it varied in each case—their policy decisions were made by individual rulers. Individuals have their peculiarities. Insofar as kings and queens made policy—and historians differ as to the extent to which they did in the years in question—policies were affected by personal prejudices, objectives, and quirks.

Academic historians tend to focus on the impersonal forces that shape history; and to ignore the sometimes decisive effect of rulers at a time when kings still ruled. *Royalty and Diplomacy in Europe 1890–1914*, by Roderick R. McLean, cited in the bibliography, is one work that provides a useful corrective to that view. On the other hand, Kaiser William II, for example, held an exaggerated view of his power to make decisions for his empire.

So historians differ among themselves as to who made which decisions in the nineteenth century; and even at the time, as decisions were being made, actors in the drama differed among themselves as to who was responsible.

KAISER WILLIAM II, boastful and vain, believed or at least claimed to believe in the divine right of kings. His, he argued, was an absolute monarchy. This was not true; but the limits of power and responsibility in Wilhelmine Germany are subjects of continuing study and cannot easily be discerned. Willy, as we know now, had a love-hate relationship with Britain that made him, at least at the time, want to be more English than the English. Queen Victoria's policy—which at times was more a family policy than a foreign policy—left him confused. He wanted to believe that he was Victoria's favorite grandson; but, if so, why did he want his navy to surpass hers? Since the Czar of Russia was his close relative, why did Nicky ignore his advice and refuse to put monarchical solidarity ahead of Russian interests?

One of the confusing things in studying Willy's career is this distinction that he drew repeatedly between the Russian government and its people. He sees the Czar and his family as Germans like himself and as members of his and Queen Victoria's family. But the people of Russia are Slavic; and therefore, in his view, inferior. At times he feared them, apparently because of their vast numbers; and toyed (as did his generals) with the notion of a preventive war against them. In some of his conversations he talked about Teutons versus Slavs in an Armageddon sort of way, as a final battle to determine the destiny of Europe.

William must have known that the advice he gave to Czar Nicolas over the course of years was not in Nicky's best interest. His communications took the form of seventy-five letters, written by the Kaiser in English longhand, begun when Nicky took the Russian throne and continued until the start of the Great War in 1914, and published by the Russian revolutionaries in 1919. The French Ambassador in St. Petersburg somehow obtained access to some of these in 1904, at the time of the Russo-Japanese War; and they made extraordinary reading. At the time they were accounted to be mere follies of the Kaiser's own; but Clark tells us that they were vetted and revised by the German Foreign Office, as were so many documents for which Willy took the blame.[1]

Willy kept telling Nicky to send his forces back into the fray in a conflict that was proving to be very one-sided. Ian Dunlop, who has written an excellent biography of Edward VII, gives a particularly detailed account of Willy's disastrous urgings.[2] The Kaiser flattered the Czar outrageously, much as Roosevelt later flattered the Kaiser.

"Do you know how we will call ourselves henceforth, you and I?" asked Willy of Nicky. "I will call you 'Admiral of the Pacific' and you will call me 'Admiral of the Atlantic.'"[3]

When the Russo-Japanese War started in 1904, the Japanese destroyed the Russian fleet in Japanese waters. So the Kaiser urged "Dearest Nicky" to send out a second fleet. Russia did so; and the second fleet blundered into disaster. On its first night out in October 1904 it encountered a few British fishing trawlers off what is known as the Dogger Bank. Unaccountably, the Russian commanding admiral mistook them for Japanese torpedo boats and opened fire on them, sinking one with its crew and devastating others. Making no effort to pick up survivors, the Russians continued on their way, taking the long route, going around Africa, and finally reappearing in May 1905 in Japanese waters. There the Russian fleet was totally destroyed by the Japanese.

All around the world there was condemnation of the Russians for not aiding the British survivors of Dogger Bank. In London there was strong support for sending the Royal Navy after the Russians to sink them; but then the Japanese did it for them. Even the Prince of Wales was caught up for a time against the Russians—until he calmed down and remembered that Britain and France would need Russia's help against Germany.

NICHOLAS II BECAME CZAR of Russia in 1894. He was only twenty-six years old. His father thought him singularly unfit to rule, and three years earlier had remarked: "He is nothing but a boy, whose judgments are childish."[4] On his accession to the throne, William II undertook to guide and advise his young relative. Clearly he believed that Nicholas held plenary power in the Russian Empire. Theoretically that was true, but in practice it was not. Professor McLean tells us that "Nicholas did not even have a private secretary."[5] He lacked the machinery to control a government.

Nicholas quickly came to resent advice from William. William, however, misunderstood. The Prussian King continued to believe that the Russian Czar, when it came to a showdown, would choose monarchical solidarity over the interests of Russia: that he would put family ahead of country. William counted on Nicholas to desert the

Russian alliance with republican France. Nicholas would not—and probably could not—do so.

SEEKING AN ALLIANCE with Russia, the Kaiser met with his cousin, the Czar, in the summer of 1905. William was aboard his royal yacht *Hohenzollern*; Nicholas was aboard his royal yacht *Polar Star*. The two vessels cast anchors in the Gulf of Finland near a fishing village named Björkö. The purpose of the meeting was a closely guarded secret. The two autocrats dined aboard *Polar Star*.

William was playing at lone-hand diplomacy, as he loved to do. His object was to get Nicholas's signature on a treaty of alliance. Russia had just disastrously lost its war with Japan, and William's calculation was that the Czar, dealing from weakness, might want German military protection. What William ignored was that Russia was tied to France by a vital need for French financing.

Happily, William collected his cousin's signature on the treaty. Then the two emperors left the Gulf of Finland and returned, so to speak, to real life. There the German and Russian governments disavowed the treaty. Abjectly apologizing to Chancellor von Bülow for acting without him, William pleaded with Bülow not to resign in protest: Bülow, he wrote, was "100,000 times more valuable to me . . . than all the treaties in the world." Threatening suicide and displaying a rare light touch, he said: "Think of my poor wife and children."[6]

IN A LETTER TO THE Prince of Wales, William boasted, "I am the sole master of German policy and my country must follow wherever I go."[7] As noted earlier, the debate among scholars continues as to the

*Russian Tsar Nicolas II meets German Kaiser Wilhelm
II. France watches mistrustfully through the window.*

precise extent of William's personal rule once he was crowned. Ironically, several of the decisions for which historians most blame him
are those in which he was right but allowed himself to be overruled
by his government.[8]

What is undeniable is that William's whole view of Great Power
foreign policy over the course of two decades was colored by his
undying hatred of the Prince of Wales, his uncle who became King
of England.

A German diplomat who had occasion to observe both men over
many years believed that the personal vanity of the two made it difficult for them to get along.[9] Roderick McLean claims that their en-

mity really was a by-product of the Kaiser's hatred of his mother, who was Bertie's favorite sister.[10] Supposedly there was a quarrel— of which we know nothing—in November 1881, during a visit to Sandringham (one of Bertie's residences) by Willy.

Going back to the 1880s, a theory that some historians find persuasive is that the feud arose from the proposed marriage of Prince Alexander von Battenberg to Willy's sister Victoria ("Moretta"), who was Bertie's niece and Queen Victoria's granddaughter. Victoria, Vicki, Fritz, and Bertie proposed the marriage. Bismarck, who was still Germany's Chancellor at the time, and his government strongly opposed it. Willy, as was his custom, sided with his grandfather against his mother and father and, Professor Clark tells us, "supplied his grandfather with reports of secret meetings between his sister"—the proposed bride—and the proposed groom.[11] The quarrel grew into a more general feud between the two men and their families. It widened year after year. A year later Willy warned the Czar of Bertie's "false and intriguing character."[12]

Willy's wife Dona also was strongly opposed to the Prince—and Princess—of Wales; on a personal level, she detested Alix.

The German royal couple strongly disapproved of the free life led by Bertie and by the Marlborough House set of which he was the leader—and which Alix accepted.

Bertie, in turn, was revolted by Willy's treatment of his mother (Bertie's sister) after Fritz, his father, died. "His conduct towards you is simply revolting," he told her; "But alas! He lacks the feelings and usages of a gentleman!"[13]

To her Prime Minister, Lord Salisbury, Queen Victoria worried that Willy's conduct might interfere with the normal conduct of political relationships, saying, "this might at any moment become impossible."[14]

. . .

PHILIPP ZU EULENBURG, for a period of time before and after 1900, was the Kaiser's best friend and intimate political adviser. He therefore was privy to the thinking of the German government in the prewar era. In 1919, reflecting on what had caused the First World War, he focused on two factors: the conflict between the Prince of Wales, later Britain's King Edward VII, and Kaiser William II; and Britain's attempted encirclement of Germany. The feud was something the Kaiser had brought on himself. The encirclement was something the German government had brought on itself when it refused to renew the Reinsurance Treaty.

Fitfully, the royal families of Germany and Britain, or their governments, would attempt a reconciliation. Nothing came of these efforts. In February 1901, after the burial of Queen Victoria, Kaiser William delivered a speech in which he said that Germany and Britain ought to form an alliance: "with such an alliance not a mouse could stir in Europe without our permission."[15] Carried away by his own rhetoric, Willy might well have believed that at the time. But it was typical of him to make a large proposal in a fit of enthusiasm and then to provide no follow-through.

The nearest thing to a consistent view that Willy held throughout his life was his hatred of his uncle Bertie. He allowed this to affect his views on foreign policy. Bertie, on the other hand, seemed to make a conscious effort to keep the feud from affecting his judgment, or England's policies.

THE ROLE OF ROYALTY in forming policy was, in any event, quite different in the United Kingdom than it was in Germany. When

Queen Victoria ascended the throne, she was a mere girl, and—wisely for the most part—she leaned on the worldly Whig grandee Lord Melbourne for advice.

The extent of the Queen's power in relation to that of the Cabinet was the subject of a running negotiation throughout the nineteenth century; but the balance of power tipped noticeably towards the Cabinet after Prince Albert died and Victoria withdrew from much of public life.

As seen earlier, Victoria excluded her eldest son almost entirely in respect of government and politics, until he was fifty years old; and he did not ascend the throne until he was sixty.

Leaders of both political parties deplored this, and urged Victoria to apprentice Bertie in order to prepare him for the duties he might well have to assume one day; but she refused.

In the course of his life, Bertie fell ill at least twice with a malady that might have proved fatal. It is not inconceivable that the Queen seriously intended to outlive the Prince of Wales in hopes of providing Britain with a more suitable successor to herself.

As it was, the pursuit of pleasure did not fully occupy Bertie's time and attention. He took a keen interest in politics, and especially in foreign policy. With his easy access to the leading men of the day, he was able to make himself outstandingly well informed. He met with Léon Gambetta, the French republican leader, and with Sir Charles Dilke, an English politician who advocated abolition of the British monarchy. Free of prejudice—and he *was* free of prejudice—he moved easily in groups and classes that establishment figures never saw or heard. The Rothschilds and other Jewish bankers who became regular members of his social set were able to supply the latest and most accurate foreign intelligence.

After a time, he knew "everyone." At one point in the 1880s,

London was sending out a man to Constantinople. He was a new man. Bertie suggested that instead of going straight to the Turkish capital, he might stop along the way to get acquainted with local leaders to whom Bertie could offer his introduction. Britain's Foreign Secretary, Lord Salisbury, agreed. "The Prince of Wales is a thorough man of the world and knows all those individuals personally."[16] The Prime Minister, Benjamin Disraeli, concurred.

Bertie traveled all the time. Foreign leaders confided in him freely; he, after all, was "family." At home and abroad, it may have been assumed (wrongly) that Queen Victoria and her Cabinet kept him fully informed—so that it was safe to tell him what he must already know.

One of the royal privileges that Bertie shared with his family had to do with appointments. Bertie was able to push his favorites into key positions. This was notably true at the Foreign Office, where the interests of Charles Hardinge and his set were moved ahead: officials who believed that France had become England's friend and Germany its enemy.

Even when he became King, Bertie did not make foreign policy for his country. He contrived nonetheless to make himself a political figure of some consequence who wielded considerable influence in the affairs of Britain and the world. Certainly the diplomatic corps believed so. Indeed it was the informed opinion of Paul Metternich, German Ambassador to London (in 1905), that the key to reconciliation between Germany and Britain was mediation between Emperor William and King Edward, and that it would be necessary "since both these monarchs have so great a personal influence on policy, to induce them to forget their differences."[17]

PART FOUR

A PROFILE OF
TEDDY

16 TEEDIE REFUSES TO BE WEAK

A PLAQUE STILL VISIBLE in Manhattan marks the spot where America's first President Roosevelt lived. It is at 28 East Twentieth Street, in the Gramercy Park district: then, as now, a wealthy and privileged section of town. One might find a certain irony in the observation that a foe of concentrated wealth should have emerged from that particular address. Ironies abounded in Roosevelt's life and career.

More, perhaps, than most people, Theodore Roosevelt Junior ("Teedie" to his family) was a jumble of contradictions. The future President and champion of the ordinary man was born as close to an aristocrat as an American can get. Indeed, in supplying the outlines of his life, he stressed his genealogy: "I was born in New York, October 27, 1858; my father of old dutch knickerbocker stock; my mother was a Georgian, descended from the revolutionary Governor Bullock."[1] In both cases Teddy felt pride of birth.

On his father's side, Teddy emerged from generations of wealth. They were merchants. Teddy's grandfather was a millionaire with extensive real estate holdings. On his mother's side, however, he descended not from merchants but from warriors.

Their household was split, as were so many American families, by the Civil War. Martha ("Mittie"), Teddy's mother, was a Southerner, from Georgia; his father, Theodore Roosevelt Senior ("Thee") was a New Yorker and a Federal Union man. New York was at war with Georgia. Passions ran high. Loyalties were deeply felt. New Yorkers, like the citizens of other states, sacrificed; suffered; and learned to live with their losses. Georgia, however, became a special case when the conflict drew to a close: the state went up in flames when the armies of the North—Sherman's armies—marched through it to the sea, cutting the southern Confederacy in two, and putting its plantation society to the torch.

Mittie, one of life's invalids, pleaded her neurasthenia to insist that her husband buy his way out of military service. This was quite legal then. Mittie claimed that she could not stand to think of her husband fighting her brothers—and her plea was granted.

Maybe it should not have been. She may have been someone who made herself helpless in order to occupy her husband's time and attention—or to get her own way. Lively, imaginative, delicate, whimsical, funny, at times a tease, she once was described by a female cousin as "the wildest girl she had ever known."

She regaled her children with tales of her ancestors who now were theirs: of lovers and warriors and adventurers. This suggests a Zelda Fitzgerald; but Mittie, unlike Zelda, was well this side of sanity.

However, her husband, Thee, suffered lifelong guilt from his failure, because of her, to go to war. Not merely did it disturb him; it disturbed Teedie. Thee loved Teedie more than his other three children. Teedie worshipped Thee. He also feared him. He admitted that his father was "the only man of whom I was ever really afraid."[2]

Yet in at least one respect the idol proved to have feet of clay. War, in Teedie's lifelong view, was the ultimate test of manhood; and his father had not met it.

TEEDIE CHOSE SIDES. Between his mother, who either was, or played, the helpless female, and his manly father, young Theodore Roosevelt Junior chose to follow in his father's path. His mother represented invalidism: it defined what he deplored. But starting in 1862, when he was only three years old, Teedie fell victim to debilitating and potentially fatal asthma. He suffered from asthmatic and bronchitic attacks from then on. According to his recent biographer, Kathleen Dalton, these attacks "began to dominate" his childhood.[3] Nor did they stop; they continued the rest of his life.

So the invalidism that he despised so much in his mother's inheritance was within himself. The goal of his life was to overcome weakness. He refused to make any concessions to it. He would push himself to the limit—and beyond it. In nearly everything that he would do in life he would go all the way. He was more than exuberant; he was reckless. Again and again he would take risks that hardly seemed sane. He was determined not to show weakness.

He persuaded the world that by sheer power of will, or by exercise, or by fighting back, he had defeated the illness. He had cured himself, he claimed. The world—which mostly believed what Theodore Roosevelt told it about himself—believed that he had done so. It was a central part of his persona: of the TR myth.

It was not that he did not try. At Harvard College—the school that Roosevelts attended—he threw himself into vigorous exercise programs of his own devising. They helped, but not enough. Whether or not he became the first American president to be less than candid about his health, he certainly was not the last: one thinks of Woodrow Wilson, of Franklin D. Roosevelt, and of John F. Kennedy.

The truth, as revealed by one of his sisters after his death, was that his asthma attacks became less frequent as time went on, but that they never entirely ceased.[4]

17 TEEDIE IN LOVE

TEEDIE'S HOME VALUES remained with him always. They formed a strict code. He believed in marriage, family, and monogamy. By temperament as well as by belief he was faithful. He was loyal to friends and to family members. He was a gentleman, not merely where women were concerned, but where anyone was concerned.

Historians have remained all the more puzzled by the curious turn that his relationship took with his childhood sweetheart. She was Edith Kermit Carow, a playmate of the Roosevelt children. (TR was the second of four children.) When Teedie and his siblings were taken by their father on a Grand Tour of Europe—Teedie was about eleven years old at the time—it was Edith who symbolized for him what he was leaving behind; he wrote, "Her face stired [*sic*] up in me homesickness and longings for the past which will come again never, alack never."[1]

Edith's father, born to the same social set as Teedie's father, failed in business and disintegrated in bouts of alcoholism. Edith took school lessons with the Roosevelt children and joined in their group. Corinne, one of Teedie's sisters, became her best friend; but, Kathleen Dalton tells us, it was Teedie with whom she shared books and dreams. Dalton, his sensitive and most recent biographer, quotes Roosevelt as saying that he "greatly liked the girls' stories" that he and Edith read together, though it apparently disturbed him that this taste of his was "at the cost of being deemed effeminate."

Roosevelt Senior was pushing Teedie to overcome his asthmatic invalidism and to become more manly; while Edith's mother was looking ahead to the time when one of the young men Edith knew might be eligible to secure her future. But for the moment at least, Edith did not care for these others. She adored Teedie. Dalton tells us that Edith kept a lock of Theodore's hair in her jewelry box.[2]

AT HARVARD TEEDIE, taught by his father to remain "pure," was considered something of a prig. He made himself, as best he could, in his father's image. "Thee," at the time, was engaged in the attempt to reform the American government's civil service. It was a losing fight. He had been on the winning side of the Hayes-Tilden presidential election, and had been appointed by Hayes to the New York Customs House. The New York political organization blocked the appointment. In the post–Civil War Gilded Age, the robber baron era, the government of the United States was hopelessly corrupt. The big cities were ruled by boss-led political machines that dispensed jobs, welfare, and favors. They controlled votes, from the local level to that of the presidency.

In February 1878 Thee died. It was a terrible blow to Teedie. He was only nineteen at the time. He wept; he sought counsel; he resolved that "with the help of my God I will try to lead such a life as

Father would have wished me to do."[3] His sentiment was something like Queen Victoria's when Albert died.

Edith Carow was only seventeen, but she was one of those whose advice he sought. Among friends there were those who had long expected that one day they would marry. But in August 1878 they quarreled. Nobody knows what happened. He was young, in deep emotional need, and out of control. She was under enormous pressures arising from her father's drinking and his money problems. The two parted in bitter anger. He galloped away, pushing his mount; Dalton tells us that "when a neighbor's dog barked at him as he rode by, he pulled out his revolver and shot it."[4]

IN OCTOBER 1878 a classmate introduced Teedie to a cousin: Alice Hathaway Lee, a gorgeous seventeen-year-old blonde, heiress to a banking fortune, and a figure in Boston high society: someone related to Cabots and Lowells.

Determined to wed her, he threw himself at her. When he scented a rival, he challenged the young man to a duel. He got into a fight; he went on a hunting expedition; he climbed a mountain; he was miserable; he drank; he could not sleep. Later he could see that he was "pretty nearly crazy" over Alice.[5] He proposed marriage to her often, and as often was rejected. He attacked her as though she were an enemy fortress to be taken by storm.

One can only wonder at the maturity of a teenage girl who was able to deal with such madness. As it was, with the passage of time, Teedie brought himself back under control. He integrated himself into Alice's family. He calmed down. He assured her and reassured her. He promised her not to be jealous or possessive. In the end, he won Alice's consent. On his twenty-second birthday he wed Alice, just emerging from her teens.

Before the wedding, Roosevelt's physician advised him that his heart condition was dangerous: that he must not exert himself or he might die. The young man paid no attention. He continued his exercises, and celebrated his coming wedding by chopping down trees.

ODDLY, ROOSEVELT FOUND himself replicating the marriage of his parents. Alice was like his mother: she leaned on him. She was dependent on him for almost everything, seeing in that her role as a wife. Of course that resulted in claims being made on his time and attention: claims that interfered with his search for a career. He had enrolled in the Columbia Law School and contemplated public service of some sort. His wife's constant calls on him, like his mother's, were occasionally tedious: he no longer took the two women entirely seriously when they claimed their cries were urgent.

February 1884. Valentine's Day. A daughter was born to Theodore and Alice. It should have been a cause for rejoicing. Instead, ironically, it was the occasion of the bitterest tragedy of his life. To compound the disaster, he had been warned in advance—and had paid no heed. Messages from home should have alerted him to the impending crisis: both his mother and his wife were in mortal danger.

Instead of taking the warnings seriously, he dismissed them as the usual exaggerations of his womenfolk. He had not even come home for his daughter's birth: he was busy. So there was nothing to cushion the blow for him; within hours of each other, his mother had died of typhoid and his wife had died in childbirth. And he had not believed them!

Left behind was a newborn daughter, whom Theodore was unable to rear on his own. As so often when he was in need, Theodore turned to his oldest sister, Anna, known as "Bamie" (for "bambino"). He threw himself into activity, trying to somehow put the double tragedy out of his mind. He appeared to be at his all-time low. Curiously, he recovered soon.

At Bamie's house on Madison Avenue, he encountered Edith, his long-ago girl next door. As Victorians did, he had pledged to remain faithful to Alice: to never remarry. But it looks very much to have been a union of two souls destined for each other; and six weeks later they decided to wed. Their engagement was to be kept a secret until the following year.

18 WHAT SHOULD HE DO WITH HIS LIFE?

A MAN—even one of independent means—should have a job: such was a belief handed down by Roosevelts and others of similar class and clan. Yet Theodore Roosevelt Junior had never known a sense of vocation. He had been too ill to attend school until he enrolled in Harvard College. As a child, though, he had taken an interest in the out-of-doors. In his memoirs he paints an appealing picture of his family life at that time. He tells us that "we children, of course, loved the country beyond anything. We disliked the city. We were always wildly eager to get to the country when spring came, and very sad when in the late fall the family moved back to town."[1] In his memory, the countryside was an idyllic place, filled with "all kinds of pets—cats, dogs, rabbits, a coon, and a sorrel Shetland pony named General Grant . . . a round of uninterrupted and enthralling pleasures—supervising the haying and harvesting, picking apples, hunting frogs successfully and woodchucks unsuccessfully, gathering hickory-nuts and chestnuts for sale to patient parents . . . "[2]

The sight of a dead seal displayed in a Manhattan market made him decide to study zoology. "As long as that seal remained there I haunted the neighborhood of the market day after day. I measured it, and I recall that, not having a tape measure, I had to do my best to get it with a folder pocket foot-rule, a difficult undertaking. I carefully made a record of the utterly useless measurements, and at once began to write a natural history of my own, on the strength of that seal."[3]

Roosevelt's younger sister, Corinne, later recounted how when Teedie prepared to leave on a trip, he "advertised and offered the large sum of ten cents for every field-mouse and thirty-five cents for a family."[4]

Roosevelt's love for nature, however, was not matched by his ability. ("Quite unknown to myself I was, while a boy, under a hopeless disadvantage in studying nature. I was very near-sighted, so that the only things I could study were those I ran against or stumbled over.")[5]

Posterity's image of Roosevelt is of a young person who triumphed over frailties. He himself sometimes came close to admitting that he learned to live with them rather than to overcome them.

He wrote that

> For reasons which I am wholly unable to explain even to myself I somehow rather shrink from having a sketch of my younger days prepared. . . . I was a rather sickly, rather timid little boy . . . and not excelling in any form of sport. Owing to my asthma I was not able to go to a school, and I was nervous and self-conscious, so that as far as I can remember my belief is that I was rather below than above my average playmate in point of leadership.[6]

Again:

> I did a good deal of boxing and wrestling at Harvard,
> but never attained to the first rank in either, even at my
> own weight. Once, in the big contests in the Gym, I got
> into either the finals or the semifinals; I forget which, but
> aside from this the chief part I played was to act as trial
> horse for some friend or classmate who did have a
> chance at distinguishing himself in the championship
> contests.

Again:

> I was fond of horseback-riding, but I took to it slowly
> and with difficulty, exactly as with boxing. It was a long
> time before I even became a respectable rider, and I
> never got much higher. I mean that I never became a
> first-flight man in the hunting field, and never even ap-
> proached the bronco-busting class in the West. Any
> man, if he chooses, can gradually school himself to the
> requisite nerve, and gradually learn the requisite seat
> and hands, that will enable him to do respectably across
> country or to perform the average work on a ranch.[7]

At Harvard, Roosevelt sought to become a professional natural-
ist, but was turned off by the university's focus on indoor work and
early microbiology. The Columbia Law School seemed a better pros-
pect; he dropped out, however, after only a year.

Of his law school experience, Roosevelt had little good to say,
though he tried to be fair.

But, doubtless chiefly through my own fault, some of the teaching of the law books and of the classroom seemed to me to be against justice. The caveat emptor side of the law, like the caveat emptor side of business, seemed to me repellent; it did not make for social fair dealing. The "let the buyer beware" maxim, when translated into actual practice, whether in law or business, tends to translate itself further into the seller making his profit at the expense of the buyer, instead of by a bargain which shall be to the profit of both. It did not seem to me that the law was framed to discourage as it should sharp practice, and all other kinds of bargains except those which are fair and of benefit to both sides.[8]

It was clear that he was not cut out to be a lawyer.

19 | POLITICS!

TEDDY, WHEN FIRST MARRIED, settled with Alice in the upper-class section of Manhattan known as the Silk Stocking district. He registered as a Republican. In the local Republican clubhouse, his patrician name entitled him to move to the head of the line as a potential clean-government reform candidate for public office. Soon an opportunity presented itself.

Teddy dropped out of law school to take a chance on running for the New York State Assembly. He won, and took his seat in 1881 as a Republican.

In New York at the time, and in Massachusetts, as in similar states of the industrializing northeast of the United States, the big cities tended to be run by Democratic political machines that were attacked by Republican candidates in the name of clean government. The Theodore Roosevelts, father and son, were crusading reformers of this sort. Indeed almost as soon as Teddy took his seat in the Assembly, it became clear that he was his father's son.

Roosevelt's younger sister, though perhaps biased in her assessment, claimed, "Already, by the end of a month or so [as an assembly-man], he was known as 'the Young Reformer,' ardent and earnest, who pleaded for right thinking and definite practical interpretation of right thinking."[1] She also saw that he was an American nationalist.

Early in his legislative career, Roosevelt announced that he would speak at the prestigious, elite 19th Century Club on "Americanism," while a newspaper editor would respond. Roosevelt's initial speech left the audience cold, and another speaker offered a rebuttal, alleging that "Americanism," like spiritualism or hypnotism, was a fad "ism." When Roosevelt came to give his final statements, however, "he leaned far over from the platform" and struck home:

> "I believe that I am allowed ten minutes in which to re-fute the arguments of my opponent. I do not need ten minutes—I do not need five minutes—I hardly need one minute—I shall ask you one question, and as you answer that question, you will decide who has won this argument—myself or the gentleman on the other side of this platform. My question is as follows: if it is true that all isms are fads, I would ask you, Fellow Citizens, what about PATRIOTISM?"

The audience rose to its feet in his support.

His crusades against corruption in government were less well received, especially in the press. "His strong point is his bank account, his weak point is his head,"[2] said one paper, linking his class and wealth to his implied lack of brains. "The popular voice of New York will probably leave this weakling home hereafter." The sugges-tion, presumably, was that he would be denied reelection—but that proved not to be the case.

Roosevelt's star rose in his third term, as he attacked the corruption of Tammany Hall, the crooked political machine of Manhattan. Cartoons pictured him favorably: one "with a huge pair of scissors clipping the claws of the Tammany Tiger; another as Ajax defying the corrupt influences behind police corruption; another as a woodman cutting down a huge tree of municipal graft and rascality . . ."[3]

Teddy was virtuous, but he was more than that. His life in the early 1880s provides clues to the complexities of his character. It was then that he first encountered Henry Cabot Lodge, who became his closest friend and political partner. In Lodge he was to find an alter ego: they formed a two-man team that sought to understand America's interests and America's destiny. The closer they felt that they came to finding answers to their questions, the more they became aware of the odds against them; for few Americans in their time sympathized with their point of view. It was, in a way, two against the world: a cabal of two.

". . . I never make friends at all easily," Teddy told Lodge and Lodge's wife, Anna ("Nannie"); "outside of my own family you two are really the only people for whom I genuinely care."[4] Lodge was an older man, more experienced, and more accomplished than Roosevelt. He was a professional academic historian. His biographer William C. Widenor reminds us that Lodge was "one of the three young men to receive from Harvard the first Ph.D.'s in history ever granted in the United States."[5] His teacher was Henry Adams, a witness to American history who had the benefits of a European influence and education. The famous intellectual set that grew up around Adams, and to some extent his brother Brooks, provided an open house in Washington, D.C., in the 1880s and 1890s, for Lodge and, on its fringes, for Roosevelt.

.   .   .

IT WOULD HAVE BEEN easy to foresee a career for Teddy as someone who would walk in his father's footsteps: someone of inherited
wealth and inherited principles. He could have been the sort of candidate who disdains compromise because he has no personal need to
accomplish anything; who never conquers because he never stoops
to do so; whose aim in politics is to convince mankind that the only
reason he loses the game is that he refuses to play it.

Roosevelt headed the New York delegation to the Republican
National Convention of 1884. There he fought to nominate a reform
candidate for the presidency—but lost. Instead the party ran James
Blaine, the very type of a politician who sells government favors.
True believers deserted to the Democratic candidate, Grover Cleveland, and were shocked when Roosevelt did not join them; and some
blamed it on the influence of Henry Cabot Lodge. That was not true;
but what *was* true was that their standing together for Blaine in the
1884 presidential election proved to be the beginning of an intimate
friendship that was instrumental in bringing Roosevelt to the political
heights. Both men believed in regular party loyalty as one of the keys
to political success.

According to Lodge's biographer Widenor, "Part of the extraordinary intimacy of Lodge and Roosevelt was due to the fact that for
so long they had only each other."[6] They schemed together and
helped one another: it was a case of one-plus-one-equals-three. Both
men were keenly aware that it would be politically imprudent for
them to fully express to the public the imperialist views they held in
common. "Lodge and Roosevelt," as Widenor tells us, "were to suffer many reverses in their efforts to get the American people to accept
their version of America's future."[7] That version was not always easy

to define. It owed much to the intellectual legacy of Alexander Hamilton, of the Federalist Party, and of John Quincy Adams; and both men were deeply conscious that, New York and Massachusetts aristocrats that they were, this was a heritage that flowed through their veins.

They advocated an assertive nationalism that aimed at national greatness, but were in search of an ideology that would enable them to realize it. According to Widenor, "It was five years from 1890 when Mahan sent [Lodge] a complimentary copy of 'The Influence of Sea Power upon History' to 1895 . . . when he took up the whole Mahan philosophy."[8]

Meanwhile Lodge had taken a major step up the ladder of American politics. At the beginning of 1893, the Massachusetts legislature elected him to the United States Senate—for in those days senators were not chosen by popular vote. At once he began efforts to pull Roosevelt up behind him.

Lodge and Roosevelt were consciously in quest of an ideology for a changing America in a changing world. As Widenor tells us, "It was a lonely search."[9]

Their political positions were unequal. When they met, Roosevelt was a mere State Assemblyman, while Lodge was about to become a United States Senator. Both bore famous family names, but Lodge was on the verge of being a national figure in the Republican Party, while Roosevelt remained a local one.

The pattern of their teamwork in the last two decades of the nineteenth century was one in which Lodge promoted the fortunes of Roosevelt. Lodge was the inside man in politics, while Roosevelt was the public man. This arrangement suited the talents of both. Teddy had enthusiasm, spontaneity, and a willingness, when necessary, to risk making a fool of himself. He had made himself into an effective campaigner; while Lodge, immensely clubbable, was accumulating power and chits in Washington. And where other New York and Massachusetts politicians of their era pursued personal advancement for its own sake, the two friends, true to their family heritages, sought to serve higher goals.

20 FOLLOWING THE WESTERN STAR

IN THE EARLY 1880S, Teddy had picked up and put down the several possibilities that lay before him. He experimented with different kinds of studies. He gave up science for law, and law for politics. The tragic death of his gorgeous young first wife removed what might have been a distraction from his career accomplishments; while his second marriage provided him with a helpmeet who was in truth helpful.

In 1883 he tried his hand at money making by investing in a cattle-ranching business in the Dakota Territory. Shortly afterward he traveled out West himself, to inspect the business, and perhaps to complete himself as a person; for in those days Americans believed in the redemptive powers of the West.

America began in the fifteenth century as a quest; and although Columbus did not find what he was looking for, he found the answers to much else. In life and in literature, Europeans were given a second chance by resettling in what became the United States. From 1776 onward, it became an American commonplace that the New World provided a principled kind of politics that could serve as a model and as a cleanser for the Old World with its corruptions.

European and U.S. literature alike pictured the North American continent as virgin, innocent, untouched, and unpolluted. As time and industrialization went on, the focus shifted. It was the West—the wild, untamable West—that continued to symbolize the American promise, the endlessly expanding frontier, and the horizons that always summoned.

Europeans, it was widely believed, were creatures of their ancestry, bound by their status and shaped by their upbringing; but Americans, it often was said, invented themselves—or in any event invented illusions about themselves. In fiction, F. Scott Fitzgerald's Jay Gatsby was to become the symbolic American who manufactured himself in pursuit of a dream.

In real life it was Theodore Roosevelt who did that. At the crossroads of his life, in the early 1880s, Teddy went West to become a cattle rancher. He was a businessman. He was not one of the business's cowboy employees; but a legend was born, and despite his disclaimers, persisted.

CORINNE, ROOSEVELT's younger sister, wrote that

> Although he returned to the assembly [after the deaths of Alice and Mittie] in February, 1884, and with his usual courage finished his year of duty there, he turned gladly to the new life of the West, and became, through his absolute comprehension of the pioneer type of the cowboy and the ranch-man, not only one of them from a

physical standpoint, but also one of them from the standpoint of understanding their mental outlook.[1]

William Thayer, one of Teddy's biographers, later wrote that

> Roosevelt determined . . . to devote himself to a ranchman's life. He was still in deep grief at the loss of his wife and of his mother; there was no immediate prospect of usefulness for him in politics; the conventions of civilization, as he knew them in New York, palled upon him; a sure instinct whispered to him that he must break away and seek health of body and heart and soul among the remote, unspoiled haunts of primeval Nature.[2]

Roosevelt's ranches were in the Dakotas. In writing later about his experiences there, he pointed out the dangers Westerners faced.

> When I went West, the last great Indian wars had just come to an end, but there were still sporadic outbreaks here and there, and occasionally bands of marauding young braves were a menace to outlying and lonely settlements. Many of the white men were themselves lawless and brutal, and prone to commit outrages on the Indians.[3]

> It was still the Wild West in those days, the Far West . . . [it] has gone now . . . gone to the isle of ghosts and of strange dead memories. It was a land of vast silent spaces, of lonely rivers, and of plains where the wild

game stared at the passing horseman. In that land we led
a free and hardy life, with horse and with rifle.[4]

To the elegant Cabot Lodge, attired for Boston and Washington
functions, Teddy wrote:

> Little Missouri, Dakota, August 12, 1884
>
> ... You would be amused to see me, in my broad
> sombrero hat, fringed and beaded buckskin shirt, horse-
> hide chaparajos or riding trousers, and cowhide boots,
> with braided bridle and silver spurs.[5]

*A 1906 cartoon depicting President Roosevelt as a
Rough Rider.*

To his older sister he wrote:

> having a glorious time and am well-hardened now. (I
> have just come in from spending *thirteen* hours in the
> saddle.) For every day I have been here I have had my
> hands full.[6]

He wrote that he lacked talent, but that he tried harder in order
to keep up with the other cowpunchers.

One contemporary and friend of Roosevelt's wrote:

> Even more dangerous than pursuing a stampeding herd
> at night over the plains, and plunging into the Little Mis-
> souri after it, was intercourse with some of the lawless
> nomads of that pioneer region. Nomads they were,
> though they might settle down to work for a while on
> one ranch, and then pass on to another; the sort of crea-
> tures who loafed in the saloons of the little villages and
> amused themselves by running amuck and shooting up
> the town. These men, and indeed nearly all of the pio-
> neers, held the man from the civilized East, the "tender-
> foot," in scorn. They took it for granted that he was a
> weakling, that he had soft ideas of life and was stuck-up
> or affected. Now Roosevelt saw that in order to win
> their trust and respect, he must show himself equal to
> their tasks, a true comrade, who accepted their code of
> courage and honor. The fact that he wore spectacles was
> against him at the outset, because they associated spec-
> tacles with Eastern schoolmasters and incompetence.

They called him "Four Eyes," at first with derision, but
they soon discovered that in him they had no "tender-
foot" to deal with.[7]

Easterners like Roosevelt who came out West underwent initia-
tions as tenderfeet. Teddy told of heading into the mountains with a
guide: a crippled old man who had open contempt for him. In the
mornings he often stayed in bed late, letting Roosevelt do the work.
Coming back late one day, Roosevelt found that he had drunk the
bottle of whiskey that had been brought along for (if needed) me-
dicinal purposes. Roosevelt fired the guide on the spot and started to
divide up the supplies, taking one of the horses. But the guide cocked
his rifle and refused to let either of the horses go. Roosevelt snatched
up his own rifle and got the drop on the guide, crying out, "Hands
up!" "I was only joking," said the guide. But Roosevelt did not believe him, and returned to camp, having proved that he was no ten-
derfoot.

Roosevelt was disarmingly open in telling of his failures. For
example, he recalled:

> One night early in my career I failed satisfactorily to
> identify the direction in which I was to go in order to
> reach the night herd. It was a pitch-dark night. I man-
> aged to get started wrong, and I never found either the
> herd or the wagon again until sunrise, when I was
> greeted with withering scorn by the injured cow-
> puncher, who had been obliged to stand double guard
> because I failed to relieve him.[8]
>
> There were other misadventures that I met with
> where the excuse was greater . . .

And he freely admitted:

> I never became a good roper, nor more than an average
> rider, according to ranch standards. Of course a man
> on a ranch has to ride a good many bad horses, and is
> bound to encounter a certain number of accidents, and
> of these I had my share, at one time cracking a rib and
> on another occasion the point of my shoulder. We were
> hundreds of miles from a doctor, and each time, as I was
> on the round-up, I had to get through my work for the
> next few weeks as best I could, until the injury healed of
> itself.[9]

He almost overdid his modesty in such remarks as:

> I never became more than a fair hunter, and at times I
> had most exasperating experiences, either failing to see
> game which I ought to have seen, or committing some
> blunder in the stalk, or failing to kill when I fired. Look-
> ing back, I am inclined to say that if I had any good
> quality as a hunter it was that of perseverance. "It is
> dogged that does it" in hunting as in many things.[10]

But with time he began to feel proud of his hunting prowess.

> While noiselessly and slowly threading our way through
> the thickest part of [a dense pine forest] I saw Merrifield,
> who was directly ahead of me, sink suddenly to his
> knees and turn half round, his face fairly ablaze with
> excitement. Cocking my rifle and stepping quickly for-

ward, I found myself face to face with the great bear, who was less than twenty-five feet off—not eight steps. He had been roused from his sleep by our approach; he sat up in his lair, and turned his huge head slowly towards us. At that distance and in such a place it was very necessary to kill or disable him at the first fire; doubtless my face was pretty white, but the blue barrel was as steady as a rock as I glanced along it until I could see the top of the bead fairly between his two sinister looking eyes; as I pulled the trigger I jumped aside out of the smoke, to be ready if he charged; but it was needless, for the great brute was struggling in the death agony; and, as you will see when I bring home his skin, the bullet hole in his skull was as exactly between his eyes as if I had measured the distance with a carpenters [*sic*] rule.[11]

In retrospect, Roosevelt was following a path that led to the political heights, but at the time he claimed to have left all that behind him.

[A]t any rate, I am doing some honest work whatever the result is and I am really pretty philosophical about success or failure now. It often amuses me when I indirectly hear that I am supposed to be harboring secret and bitter regret for my political career, when, as a matter of fact, I have hardly ever, when alone, given two thoughts to it since it closed, and have been quite as much wrapped up in hunting, ranching, and book-making as I ever was in Politics.[12]

Roosevelt sometimes served as a "deputy sheriff for the northern end of our county,"[13] tracking down horse thieves with a Winchester rifle in his arms and a copy of a Tolstoy novel in his saddlebag. His leadership legacy grew apace, and the anecdotes of his adventures would later be taken as proof of his fitness for larger things:

> On entering [a tavern one day, Roosevelt] saw a group of loafers and drinkers who were apparently terrorized by a big fellow, rather more than half drunk, who proved to be the local bully. The function of this person was to maintain his bullyship against all comers: accordingly, he soon picked on Roosevelt, who held his peace as long as he could. Then the rowdy, who grasped his pistols in his hands, ordered the "four-eyed tenderfoot" to come to the bar and set up drinks for the crowd. Roosevelt walked deliberately towards him, and before the bully suspected it, the "tenderfoot" felled him with a sledge-hammer blow. In falling, a pistol went off wide of its mark, and the bully lay in a faint. Before he could recover, Roosevelt stood over him ready to pound him again. But the bully did not stir, and he was carried off into another room. The crowd congratulated the stranger on having served him right.[14]

THEODORE ROOSEVELT was a New York investor who went West to supervise his ultimately unsuccessful investments in Dakota cattle ranches.

The ranch was a hired business and he was the owner and employer. He hired cowboys, but he himself was not a cowboy, even though he at times participated in the work of the ranches. He did have occasion to take part in law enforcement. He exaggerated the extent of time that he spent out West, claiming that he was there the "major part of seven years and off and on for nearly fifteen years . . ."[15] It looks as though he spent about three months a year there for about four years. The cold winter of 1886–1887 seemed to have killed most of his cattle; afterwards the business was liquidated at a loss.

Except for these claims as to the amount of time he spent on the ranch, Roosevelt was surprisingly self-deprecatory in describing his life out West. So far as his biographers have been able to tell, his accounts also of his cowboying were essentially truthful. Yet a more romantic version of events seems to have fixed itself in the public imagination and in that of posterity; and it was not necessarily less true.

Roosevelt had created a public persona for himself that lent itself to fantasy—or, for that matter, to caricature; for his characteristic quality was that he carried things too far. Whenever he set himself a goal, he threw himself at it, and his too-furious but ultimately successful courtship of his first wife was an early example of this pattern.

Henry Adams, the presiding intellectual of New England and transatlantic America, caught the spirit of the coming century at once. He foresaw that it would be an era of energy. He viewed the dynamos on display at the Chicago and Paris worlds fairs at the climax of the nineteenth century, and he understood that they were poised to let the genies out of the bottle. Mankind always had been limited. Electricity could release productivity in unlimited amounts more.

Young Theodore Roosevelt, who seemed to be in perpetual motion; whose animals spirits seemed to be indefatigable; and whose energies appeared to be limitless, seemed to incarnate the New World.

. . .

IN THE PRECEDING PASSAGES, Roosevelt's Western saga has been narrated largely in his own words. Among America's presidents, he is known—known even more than others—for telling his own story in his own words and giving it his own interpretation.

In writing about his cattle-ranch life, however, while telling about himself, he also was telling about the West. He was contributing to a growing body of American literature about life in the wilderness. Elegant city dwellers in New York and Boston might define the United States in terms of the frontier, but they had not necessarily been there; and from the birth of the country onward they showed a persistent interest in the life of the Wild West. Roosevelt's books satisfied their curiosity about the details of everyday life: about the craft, tools, and equipment of cowboys and other ranch hands.

Americans were avid readers of "Westerns": novels embodying a stark morality, in which a good gunman met an evil one at high noon under the empty sky of a lawless frontier town. These, and epic tales of the Indian wars, remained central to the motion pictures of the twentieth century, and continue on into the twenty-first. Intimations of these moral issues—of the showdown between good and evil, and of the struggle for survival in a lawless society—can be found in Roosevelt's later vision of the conflicts among nations.

21   BACK TO POLITICS!

IN THE PRESIDENTIAL administration of the Republican Benjamin Harrison (1889–1893), Senator Lodge secured a political position for his friend Roosevelt on the U.S. Civil Service Commission. The young reformer quickly confirmed the opinion, voiced by President Harrison, that he "wanted to put an end to all the evil in the world between sunrise and sunset."

The next political job that Lodge secured for him was President of the Board of Police Commissioners of New York City in 1895. As such, Roosevelt proved to be a colorful character: an unmistakable aristocrat in his silk cummerbund, who earned a reputation for smashing crime and corruption with a gloved but iron fist. He roamed the streets of the city by night, cracking down on opium dens, bordellos, and other houses of commercial vice; and delighting the newspaper reporters who accompanied him and found him compelling copy.

"Lodge urged TR to use his police work as a stepping-stone to statewide office, probably a Senate seat, then to aim for the presidency," we are told by Roosevelt biographer Kathleen Dalton.[1] "He advised him to keep his name before the voters."[2]

AGAIN LODGE MOVED up in national politics; in 1895 he was appointed to the Senate Foreign Relations Committee. After maneuverings on his part, he was able to secure Roosevelt's appointment as Assistant Secretary of the Navy in 1897.

Both men were drawn to the intellectual center of Washington: the home of Henry Adams, a block from the White House. Adams, the descendant of two presidents, was America's great man of letters. His coterie—he and four lifelong friends—called themselves "the Five of Hearts." They had been on close terms with every president from Abraham Lincoln onward. Sculptors and architects moved in their circle, as did great writers: Henry James, Edith Wharton, Mark Twain, Robert Louis Stevenson, and others. Their geopolitical views were shaped by Mahan as the turn of the century approached.

William McKinley, the current President, presided over an America much excited by what were regarded as continuing Spanish atrocities in Cuba. These feeling were whipped up by the newspapermen William Randolph Hearst and Joseph Pulitzer. Early in 1898 oil was poured on the flame when the U.S. battleship *Maine* exploded in the harbor of the Cuban capital city of Havana.

The President attempted to restore calm. The Secretary of the Navy, John D. Long, was also in favor of prudence. The Spanish government was almost unimaginably conciliatory—all to no avail. In the Navy Department, Roosevelt led the war party.

Working within the Navy Department, Roosevelt had managed to push ahead the career of Admiral George Dewey, and secured for him the command of the Asiatic fleet. In April 1898 Secretary Long, ailing and having left for the day, was away from his office when Roosevelt, taking charge, sent orders in all directions, ensuring readiness, famously cabling Dewey in Hong Kong to KEEP FULL OF COAL. IN THE EVENT OF DECLARATION OF WAR against Spain, with the plan of bottling up the Spanish navy and then beginning offensive operations against the Philippines. The cable was signed ROOSEVELT.

Legend had it that Roosevelt started the war. This exaggerates his role, as that one order certainly did not do so.

In fact, Roosevelt sent many cables and issued many orders. To prepare the armed forces of a modern country for a war that might break out at any moment requires an entire program of precautions, activities, and provisions for bases and supplies. A master of these details who gloried in warfare, Roosevelt threw himself into action almost as a one-man Navy Department.

The American fleet that—when war came—steamed into battle on the far side of the Pacific Ocean in 1898 was, however, tiny compared to the naval fleets of today. James Chace and Caleb Carr, historians of America's wars, write, "Of the nine American ships that steamed out of Hong Kong on April 25, 1898, none was a true battleship. Four were protected cruisers, armor-plated but still adorned with tall masts. Two were mere gunboats, highly vulnerable to artillery fire. One was a lowly cutter . . . and [there were] a pair of colliers, useless in combat."[3]

The British of Hong Kong took a dim view of Dewey's chances as they watched the flotilla steam by. They marveled at the inadequacy of the U.S. Pacific Fleet. But it steamed on to victory in the Battle of Manila Bay, and projected American power halfway around the world.

. . .

ACCORDING TO REPORTS reaching Washington from London, "no one in Britain opposed an American war with Spain."[4] Washington insiders were not surprised by this, as historian Patricia O'Toole remarks: "To Henry Adams, the new harmony between Britain and the United States was not in the least paradoxical. Germany, 'the grizzly terror,' had simply 'frightened England into America's arms.'"[5]

In the buildup toward the war with Spain, Teddy, inside the American government, was, as noted, a leader of the war party. But he did not command great visibility in public. He feared that the war might be played out without his having a chance to take a conspicuous role in it. He had long been aware that the U.S. Army was unprepared for war, even a war with Spain. President McKinley called for volunteers. Roosevelt took advantage of the offer to raise his own troops, the First U.S. Volunteer Cavalry, the "Rough Riders," initially under the command of his friend Leonard Wood, then under Roosevelt's own command. In large part its troops were Teddy's own typically various friends: socialites, Indians, a sheriff from Arizona, and others. As their commanding colonel, Roosevelt looked incongruously like a wild man restrained only by his ultracivilized Brooks Brothers uniform. He more or less ran his own show, and in appearance and perhaps in spirit it bore a certain resemblance to Buffalo Bill's Wild West Show.

22 | TEDDY'S WAR

SOLDIERING IS NOTORIOUSLY a matter of boredom, filth, and mismanagement. The weather and the terrain can be as dangerous as enemy troops. Disease and dysentery often take their toll. Long delays in which nothing happens are followed by sudden crises in which too much happens. So it was with the Rough Riders, suffocating in one-hundred-degree heat as they waited their chance to win glory for themselves and for their fearless leader.

Landing seaborne troops on an enemy-held shore often is the most perilous operation in a military campaign. Roosevelt was spared those dangers: Cuban rebels had cleared the way for the Americans. Roosevelt took it to be just further evidence of Spanish incompetence in failing to fortify the landing area.

ONWARD RODE THE Rough Riders; onward in search of their destiny. Onward they rode to victory.

Disdaining danger, even death, the rough-riding Roosevelt displayed tremendous courage in the Cuban campaign in such battles as that of Las Guásimas, San Juan Heights, and San Juan Hill. Leading the charges through a hail of fire, the cowboy colonel seemed impervious to bullets and shells. Again and again his arms carried all before them.

He rode to triumph most conspicuously in a battle for the heights known as Kettle Hill.[1] The Spaniards had fortified them heavily; and various American units were advancing only slowly and with heads down to provide shelter from enemy fire.[2] Rallying his own men, with heads up, Roosevelt led a cavalry charge uphill at a gallop to seize the high ground, dislodging the Spaniards from the heights.

ALMOST ALL OF Roosevelt's friends had thought it a mistake for him to quit the Navy Department when the Spanish War broke out. They were wrong. He was right—on many counts.

President McKinley in the beginning had tried to keep the peace. Senator Lodge had favored the Spanish War, in hopes that it might lead to American expansion within the Western Hemisphere. Theodore Roosevelt was in favor of war—any war. He believed that war would be good for Americans; and that fighting a war would be a good thing for any and every country from time to time. He supported the Spanish-American War with enthusiasm and no qualms. Indeed, he saw it as a central episode in the life of his generation of Americans. It was their affirmation of their manhood.

It was true for his country; it was true for himself. All of his life until then he had been haunted by what the classical Greeks visualized as Furies. There was his physical weakness, overcome by his life of strenuousness. There were his asthmatic attacks, never fully overcome and always there to haunt him. There was his father's payment for exemption from the Civil War.

Above all, there was the one supreme test that, in his firm belief, all manly men must meet: the test from which there can be no exemption. It was the test that can be administered only on the battle-field. It was the test of going to war.

From the Spanish War on, Roosevelt was at ease with himself. He was at ease with the memory of his father. He seemed to recognize that his countrymen did not share his belief that to be a real man a male human being must risk his life in armed combat; and he ap-peared to accept that. At the dinner table he frequently spoke only of his military exploits; and while it was a bore for his guests, it was a pleasure for him. He had set out to do one thing in his life—and he had done it!

A 1902 cartoon portrait of President Roosevelt in Vanity Fair.

ROOSEVELT WAS ONE OF those people who create themselves. He wore a mask for so long that it became his face. He had obeyed Plato's injunction to be what you wish to seem. He had preached and practiced the strenuous physical life; and in the end had come to thoroughly enjoy it. From the dawn of the twentieth century onwards, the questions for Teddy's biographers continued to be: Who was he? Who had he become?

In 1898, TEDDY WAS America's hero. He took advantage of that to run for Governor of New York: his first major political race. Despite his fame and his outsize personality, he won by only a relatively small majority. To obtain the nomination, he had reached an accommodation with New York's Republican political boss Thomas Platt; but their relationship was troubled, and Roosevelt, the maverick clean-government reformer, seemed unlikely to be run for reelection by the Republican machine. Instead an audacious plan was in the process of negotiation. Senator Lodge, whose long-term plan was to obtain the presidency for Roosevelt, discussed with Platt the possibility of running Teddy for Vice President with President McKinley in 1900.[3] For Platt, the advantage would be that it would get Teddy out of New York State, and would leave New York to Platt. To the other Republican political bosses, too, giving Roosevelt the utterly powerless figurehead job of Vice President would keep him out of the way and out of trouble. Who remembered, for example, Hannibal Hamlin, Abraham Lincoln's vice president? Or William King, John Breckinridge, Henri Wilson, William Wheeler—vice presidents all? The vice presidency was the end of the road.

The Republican organization had placed its bet on the prediction that Theodore Roosevelt was a candidate for oblivion.

PART FIVE

INTO THE TWENTIETH CENTURY

23 | ALARM!

ON JANUARY 1, 1901, Queen Victoria wrote in her journal: "Another year begun, and I am feeling so weak and unwell that I enter upon it sadly."[1] Nineteen days later, her resident physician phoned a message to the Prince of Wales suggesting that he remain in London to be near at hand. Soon afterward he went to see his mother at her residence, Osborne House, on the Isle of Wight. Asking all of her visitors to leave the room, the Queen told her physician: "I should like to live a little longer, as I have a few things to settle. I have arranged most things, but there are still some left and I want to live a little longer."[2] Bertie then left for London in order to receive the Kaiser—who, in the presence of his dying grandmother, for once behaved himself. The two men, along with other family members, returned by special train to the Isle of Wight and the Queen's bedside. The Kaiser was allowed five minutes alone with his grandmother. The end came at 6:30 p.m., January 22, 1901. The bulletin was brief: "The Queen is dead."

Bertie—Albert Edward, aged fifty-nine—now reigned. Aban-

King Edward VII and Kaiser Wilhelm II on
horseback at the funeral of Queen Victoria.

doning his German father's name, he chose to be Edward VII, with
his roots in English history. It was a way for him to come out of the
shadow of his parents, although he did not put it that way. He explained to the Accession Council at St. James's Palace that Albert was
a name which should remain forever reserved for "Albert the Good."[3]
As it turned out, Edward was a fitting choice on other grounds: the
Edward before him, King Edward VI, is now believed by modern
scholars to have been greatly underestimated.[4]

THOSE WHO HAD FOLLOWED the Prince of Wales's playboy career were concerned for Britain's future. "God help us all!" worried

Princess May of Teck, a family member.[5] Sir James Clark, one of Victoria's physicians, saw "troubles" ahead. [6] Sir Sidney Lee, Edward's future biographer, wrote that the contrast between Queen Victoria and her successor "was so great as to give rise to grave fears concerning the future trend of the British monarchy."[7]

The widespread fear was that, as gossipmongers claimed, Bertie was a dissolute wastrel, a gambler, a womanizer, not at all a serious person—and someone who, as king, would not and could not change.

In counterpoint to this view, Shakespeare centuries before had provided the pattern and example of what England now needed and hoped for and dreamed of. It was that Edward VII, like Henry V, would abandon frolics and follies and the company of Falstaffian companions, and instead prove, in a word, *royal*. And in large part that is what England got. But he did not give up his wide circle of friends, many of whom served him well; and he matured in his relationships with women. He proved to be an immensely popular and much loved king with a powerful personality, who led the peoples of Britain in the twentieth century toward friendship and collaboration with other democracies. He had taken office as Emperor of India, King of the United Kingdom, and—an innovation—"King of the British Dominions Overseas."[8] He was literally the uncle of Europe's reigning royalty—and he had the reassuring qualities of everybody's uncle.

THE NEWLY CROWNED monarch renovated Buckingham Palace, and installed electricity, lights, telephones, and modern plumbing. The Victorian age was over.

Used, as they were, to continuity and stability, the peoples of the British family of nations had worried about what might be in store for them. It turned out that their worries had been groundless.

By coincidence Americans had been going through a similar fit of nerves at about the same time.

IN THE AMERICAN elections of November 1900, William McKinley was reelected President of the United States. A former major in the Union army, he was the last Civil War veteran to serve as President. His youthful running mate, Theodore Roosevelt, had been only two years old when the Civil War broke out; there were a couple of generations between them.

The issues in the 1900 elections had been somewhat muddled. Americans, more than a little disillusioned, no longer remembered clearly why they had chosen in 1898 to go to war against Spain. American armies remained mired in an insurrection in the formerly Spanish Philippines in which, confusingly, native guerrillas fought for independence while the United States claimed to be fighting to give them freedom. The Republican administration argued that the United States was doing the right thing in the far-distant islands by at last playing a role in world affairs. The Democratic opposition seemed to want U.S. troops to shield the islands against foreign interference, but seemed to have nothing concrete to propose.

The new Republican ticket, McKinley-Roosevelt, was sworn into office in March 1901. Both candidates had campaigned vigorously to score this victory.

In Buffalo, New York, a world's fair called the Pan-American Exposition opened its gates in September 1901. It focused on the Americas: on the wonderful accomplishments of the Western Hemisphere during the nineteenth century. At the same time, it looked ahead to the great challenges that the country would face in the century ahead.

"Expositions are the timekeepers of progress." It was a striking phrase of McKinley's that he had used, oddly enough, in talking to his secretary earlier that summer. The President was the featured speaker at the Pan-American Exposition. He took as his theme the great issue before the United States: isolationism in world affairs. (This also was the great issue before the United Kingdom at the same time, which Edward VII and his ministers were facing in their own way.)

New technologies of transportation and communication had made the world one, McKinley told his audience of perhaps fifty thousand. "The same important news is read, though in different languages, in all Christendom"; and the speed of modern ocean liners had abolished distance. The Atlantic no longer separated North America from Europe. "God and man have linked the nations together," he said, and added, "No nation can longer be indifferent to any other." The conclusion, he said, was unmistakable: "Isolation is no longer possible or desirable."

The following day the President took time off to stroll through the fairgrounds and exhibitions on his own. A little before 4:10 p.m., a man approached him and shot him twice with a pistol. The man was an anarchist. He held no grudge against McKinley in particular, but was opposed to all governments and their leaders.

After a week in which hopes rose and fell, the President died in the early hours of Saturday, September 14, 1901.

Unpredictably, unpredictable Theodore Roosevelt became the twenty-sixth President of the United States: the youngest in America's history. As Mark Hanna had warned when Roosevelt had come under consideration for Vice President, only one life had stood between "that damned cowboy" and the presidency.

. . .

SENATOR LODGE, THE political patron responsible for promoting Roosevelt, also had introduced him into Henry Adams's set, which— at least as viewed from here and now—was America's leading intellectual center. The Adams and James families and their ramifications had known Teddy for two decades, had watched him in what they regarded as his childishness, and had helped to educate him—and were appalled that he had become President of the United States.

Henry James, the great American novelist, wrote, "I don't either like or trust the new President, a dangerous and ominous Jingo [a belligerent chauvinist] . . . "[9] (Roosevelt in turn did not like the novels of James, which he regarded as effete.)

"Here is America run by a schoolboy barely out of college . . . " wrote Henry Adams.[10] He claimed that TR "acts by the instinct of a school-boy at a second-rate boarding school," and that "mind, in a technical sense, he has not."

Adams also claimed that TR misunderstood why his friends were so fascinated by his presidency: "Theodore is blind-drunk with self-esteem. He has not a suspicion that we are all watching him as we would watch a monkey up a tree."[11] And Mark Twain wrote that "the President is insane."[12]

With Roosevelt as President and Edward as King, thinking people in the English-speaking world found themselves in a state somewhere between dismay and despair.

24 · A SPECIAL RELATIONSHIP

THEODORE ROOSEVELT, or "TR" as he became, had changed his mind about warfare—in large part in line with changing circumstances. Roosevelt the President was no longer the same man as the Navy Department official who had mobilized the fleet for the American war with Spain.

Now that Roosevelt had fought in a war himself—and had waged it publicly, conspicuously, and heroically—he seems to have purged himself of that particular demon. Roosevelt the President did not believe that war was a good thing. He continued to believe that it might be a necessary thing. But war could be prevented only by building up a nation's military might. To keep the peace, the United States in particular should maintain a powerful, modern, and efficient navy, suitable to its geographic and political circumstances, and should be ready at all times to defend the national interest.

For TR, the decisive geopolitical occurrence of his time was the conjunction at the turn of the century of America's war with Spain—which the United States won with diplomatic support from

London—and the British war with the Boers, which the British at first were losing, and only won in the end because the odds were so much in their favor. They had received diplomatic support from Washington.

Until then, TR had been in the American mainstream in believing the United Kingdom to be the main rival, and even enemy, of the United States. Whether in commerce and trade, or in building a navy, the British colonists who broke off in 1776 to create a new country competed with England afterwards in doing the same things the British did. As late as 1896, Roosevelt supported the threat of the Grover Cleveland administration to go to war against Britain. It also was good domestic politics: the massive German-American and Irish-American immigrant populations in the big cities happily voted anti-English.

But the politics of the globe had changed, as TR saw it, with the Spanish-American and Boer wars. Always finely attuned to the world's power politics, Roosevelt immediately went to the heart of the matter: the British Empire no longer was a threat to America—and never would be anymore.

Indeed, Britain might no longer be able, unaided, to uphold the status quo in the world. It would require the support of the United States to do so.

The threat to the European balance of power came from Germany. Challenges to the balance of power often bring major wars. So to keep the peace—and that was now President Roosevelt's goal—he would have to associate the United States with Britain.

He could do so with enthusiasm because he believed there should be a moral content to foreign policy. He was Anglophile: he viewed the cause of the English-speaking peoples to be synonymous with righteousness. He also felt strong sympathy for the French. These sympathies of his were not made clear to other nations, many of whom regarded him as neutral and impartial. On the other hand, Edward VII and his government were made aware that in all of the strategic areas of the world, the American President viewed American and British interests as identical.

Like British Foreign Secretary Lord Lansdowne and his colleagues in London, whose winding down of British commitments will be described presently, he translated a general desire for friendship between the countries into specific agreement on outstanding issues. TR, seeking England's friendship, found himself confronted by several specific issues to be resolved. Both Edward and Roosevelt had an inner circle of intimates who unofficially helped carry out policy.

The President, however, had a more difficult job. His mentor, old friend, and Secretary of State (inherited from McKinley), John Hay, fortunately was also an Anglophile. But, especially on the British side, officials did not understand Roosevelt.

The British ambassador, Sir Mortimer Durand, believed that TR was "unreliable" and was given to "impetuousness."[1] The British Foreign Secretary, Lord Lansdowne, told his Prime Minister (Arthur Balfour) that "Roosevelt terrifies me almost as much as the German Emperor."[2]

It took years for TR to persuade London to replace Durand. Lansdowne finally was replaced by Sir Edward Grey when the Liberals defeated the Conservatives in the 1904 elections. Then all could go relatively smoothly, but things continued to take time. Throughout the years of negotiations between America and England, it seems clear that the English King sympathized with Roosevelt and with America's side.

Nonetheless, it took almost the whole of Roosevelt's presidency to work through the entire list of outstanding disagreements between the United States and the United Kingdom. To deal with them, TR, in addition to members of his administration—Secretary of State John Hay and his replacement, Elihu Root, and Secretary of War William Howard Taft—turned to a network of informal contacts that included, but was not limited to, Cecil Spring Rice, an English diplomat who had been best man at TR's marriage to Edith; Arthur Lee, a British Member of Parliament; and the French and German ambassadors who will be mentioned shortly.

Among the specific issues that had to be gotten out of the way:

- America's right to fortify the Panama Canal
- A blockade by Germany and Britain of Venezuela in order to collect debts, which the United States regarded as a sort of invasion of America's sphere
- A U.S.-Canada border dispute about the frontier between Alaska and British Columbia
- The question of the Newfoundland fisheries: did Canadian regulations apply to American fishermen?

Once these and similar issues were resolved,[3] President Roosevelt would be in a position to create the entente partnership with the British Empire in world affairs that would realize what we now believe to have been his imperial vision: dominance of the world by the English-speaking peoples. That vision was reciprocated. "I entirely agree with you . . . " King Edward wrote the President, "and I look forward with confidence to the co-operation of the English-speaking races becoming the most powerful civilising factor in the policy of the world."[4] Having identical global interests, America and

Britain would find themselves on the same side of practically every issue.

As soon as Roosevelt became President, he and Edward took every opportunity to consult and exchange views with each other and, wherever it was suitable, to ask each other for help. The two leaders were determined to establish a close friendship. When Roosevelt became President, Edward spent time questioning the American Ambassador about him; asked for a photo of him; and asked for a copy of one of his books. Again and again the two communicated through one or another trusted intermediary. Almost as though it were a mantra, they repeated to each other that the interests of the English-speaking peoples were identical.

Luck, as noted earlier, had brought the crown to Edward; luck had brought TR to the presidency. Luck now brought together two leaders who fully agreed. In the words of H. W. Brands, a TR biographer, Roosevelt "acknowledged the importance of luck in his sudden ascent—his good luck in surviving the battle for Santiago, McKinley's bad luck with bullets and doctors."[5]

They could not, however, work as closely together as they would have liked. There were obstacles to be overcome in doing so. As President, TR was at that time bound not to leave the United States during his term of office; so he could not pay a personal visit to London. He could not commit his government without asking and obtaining the advice and consent of the Senate—and, practically speaking, that of a number of other important persons as well.

Similarly, Edward could make no commitments; only his government could do so. In carrying on the dialogue between President and King, trusted emissaries traveling between their respective countries had to act as messengers and go-betweens. It took fine judgment in each case to choose a go-between who would want to advance the particular cause and who had the skills to do so. In any event, messages had to be edited: Roosevelt's references to the Kaiser, for example, had to be flattering, because they might be intercepted.

But despite all difficulties, a new entente had been created: the special relationship between the United States and the United Kingdom. And it was based on an understanding that the pre-presidential TR, his political partner Senator Lodge, and their intellectual forebear John Quincy Adams, would have found entirely acceptable: the validity of the Monroe Doctrine and the dominance of the United States in the Western Hemisphere.

But Roosevelt as President was going further. He was taking the United States *out* of its hemisphere; he was exercising a reach that was global. He and King Edward were talking and acting as partners and allies, even though TR knew that neither the Senate nor the American people would agree to a partnership or an alliance.

The special relationship did not continue uninterrupted after the TR administration came to an end. But it provided a prototype; and in several of the most dramatic moments of the twentieth century, it returned.

25 | AN ENTENTE

THE BOER WAR HAD proved to be a chastening experience for England. It had revealed Britain's vulnerabilities. Isolationism no longer was feasible. Lord Salisbury, Victoria's longtime Foreign Secretary and Prime Minister, had died shortly after the Queen did; and for their successors, the question was not whether to ally but with whom. An alliance with Japan (1902) proved successful immediately when the Japanese Empire went to war against Russia (1904–1905) and won it.

For the United Kingdom, a natural ally always had seemed to be Germany. The royal family, for generations, had been German. Moreover, the strengths of the two were complementary: Germany was the leading land power, while the United Kingdom was the leading sea power. Germany's strength was focused on Europe, while Britain's lay in its global reach.

Joseph Chamberlain, Britain's Colonial Secretary, and perhaps the most powerful Cabinet minister except for the Prime Minister himself, harped on the theme that Britain needed to break out of isolation. In a speech in November 1899 he argued, "No far-seeing statesman could be content with England's permanent isolation on the continent of Europe. . . . The natural alliance is between ourselves and the German Empire. . . . Both interest and racial sentiment unite the two peoples and a new Triple Alliance between Germany and England and the United States would correspond with the tie that already binds Teutons and Anglo-Saxons."[1] But when Germany showed little enthusiasm for Chamberlain's proposal, he became embittered and anti-German.

Alliance talks between London and Berlin were held from time to time, but they foundered: Germany was unwilling to give up its naval race against Britain.

So in the first couple of years of Edward's reign, his government recognized the need for an ally, but had not yet found one in Europe. Yet the small group of foreign policy professionals in London and Paris turned increasingly towards an alignment with each other; and in London many of the most important among them, such as Charles Hardinge, had been closely associated with King Edward when he still was Prince of Wales. In the early 1900s the British Foreign Secretary met with the French ambassador in London to discuss settling all outstanding differences between their countries.

ACTUALLY THE TRANSITION to the Edwardian era in British foreign policy had begun while Queen Victoria was still alive. For more than two decades Lord Salisbury had held sway as Foreign Secretary (1878–1880, 1885–1886, 1887–1892, 1895–1900) and Prime Minister (1900–1902), but he resigned his post as Foreign Secretary in 1900 and no longer dominated policymaking in London thereafter. He resigned as Prime Minister in 1902 and died in 1903. His death severed the tie with the past. This "strange, powerful, inscrutable, brilliant" man (in the words of young Winston Churchill) had governed the global British Empire from his ancestral home at Hatfield House as though it were his country estate.[2] Now his Cabinet colleagues took matters into their own hands.

The new Foreign Secretary was Lord Lansdowne. He was widely criticized at the time for his administration of the War Office, his previous Cabinet position, having been Secretary for War at the start of the Boer War. It may have been that very experience that caused him to be aware of Britain's growing vulnerability. He was alive to the danger of isolationism in the twentieth century, as heavily armed Great Powers formed and re-formed combinations with and against each other, promiscuously and with the utmost rapidity. The new Prime Minister, Arthur Balfour, and the Cabinet supported Lansdowne in seeking to avoid the conflicts that might arise for England as a result.

From the start, Lansdowne treated the Prince of Wales, who then became Edward VII, with the greatest deference. His regard was not entirely reciprocated. Edward's assistant private secretary wondered why the King never "hit it off" with Lansdowne.[3] The answer may have been buried in the past. It probably arose from the Aylesford scandal described in chapter 10. Lansdowne had intervened in that affair in a way that Bertie had found offensive, and had used language in addressing him that the Prince of Wales had found insulting.[4] Edward VII had not forgotten.

RETRENCHMENT WAS THE ORDER of the day in London. In government circles there was a pervasive sense that Britain lacked the resources, financial and otherwise, to deal with all of the conflicts in which the United Kingdom might be involved in the dangerous new century. Commitments were reviewed with an eye towards curtailing them; budgets were monitored with a view towards reducing them.

Under Lansdowne's leadership, Britain entered into the Hay-Pauncefote Treaty with the United States, by the terms of which London recognized Washington's exclusive right to build a Panama Canal. Zara Steiner, an historian of the British Foreign Office, interprets the treaty as a recognition by Britain of "the supremacy of the Americans in Western waters . . . "[5] So it was in every corner of the world; Lansdowne reduced British exposure everywhere that he could.

Lansdowne reviewed the various disagreements in which Britain found itself involved around the globe, and attempted to resolve them in order to reduce the country's exposure to risk, or at least to lower the intensity of such conflicts as might inevitably occur. To this end, dangers were downplayed. Even Wilhelmine Germany's race to match England's navy was given, by Lansdowne, a nonthreatening interpretation—until Lord Selborne, First Lord of the Admiralty (which is to say, the civilian Cabinet Minister in charge of the Navy) warned that the German navy "is being carefully built up from the point of view of a war with us."[6] Lansdowne met opposition from his colleagues when he minimized the possibility of a threat from Germany.

But as Zara Steiner tells us, "if Edward VII had little influence on Lansdowne's diplomacy, he could still persuade the Foreign Office to accept his nominees for the senior diplomatic posts."[7]

In seeking friendship and accommodation with Germany, Lansdowne was striking out on a road of his own. In doing so, he ran counter to the advice of his Cabinet colleagues and most of his Foreign Office staff members. It was at a time when the Foreign Office was just beginning to come into its own. With Lord Salisbury gone, career officials in London saw themselves as being in a position, if not to make, then at least to influence the making of British foreign policy. A number of these officials, over the course of years, had been advanced in their careers by the Prince of Wales (as he then was). If the Foreign Office strongly influenced British policy, then the Prince (and now the King) strongly influenced the Foreign Office.

Charles Hardinge was a leading example. He was pushed forward by the Prince of Wales all along; rose steadily and quickly; and became head of the Foreign Office (1906–1910).

Others who shared the Wales point of view were Francis Bertie,[8] Louis Mallet, William Tyrrell, Reginald Lister, and Eyre Crow. According to Professor Steiner, "Through a series of intrigues, promotions, and transfers, these men succeeded to the most influential posts in London and abroad."[9]

What they had in common, to one extent or another, was a belief that Prussian-led Germany posed the greatest threat to Britain, Europe, the balance of power, and world peace that they faced as Edward mounted the throne.

In just a few years, British policymakers had come to accept that isolationism was no longer feasible for their country. They recognized that to meet threats from some Great Powers they would have to join forces with other Great Powers. King Edward looked in the direction of France. He was the scion of a German dynasty and the son of a German prince; and France had been England's main enemy for a thousand years. To back France against Germany—as Edward contemplated doing—would mean a dizzying reversal in world politics. But to Edward's following in the Foreign Office, it looked like the logical course to follow.

As for Edward: when he encountered anti-British crowds shouting slogans on the occasion of a visit to France, and someone in his party remarked, "The French don't like us," he replied, "Why should they?"[10]

IT HAS BEEN SEEN THAT, on taking office as Foreign Secretary, Lansdowne had been occupied in closing out international disputes in order to reduce Britain's vulnerabilities. The Foreign Minister of France, Théophile Delcassé, was engaged in a similar exercise at about the same time. In 1902 he and Lansdowne and Paul Cambon, French ambassador in London, met to discuss resolving one of their colonial disputes. Delcassé apparently took the initiative in offering to drop France's long-standing but hopeless objection to Britain's position in Egypt. In return he wished to obtain concessions from Britain in regard to France's claims in Morocco. But unlike Lansdowne, Delcassé was pursuing his policy because Germany, in his view, *did* pose a danger.

IT WAS IN MARCH 1903, while planning a Mediterranean cruise, that Edward had the happy thought that he might include France in his itinerary. The United Kingdom was deeply unpopular in France at the time. Imperial rivalry was responsible. France bitterly resented Britain's occupation of Egypt and the Sudan, the more so as the British had offered the French a chance to participate, which the French, unwilling at the time to take the risk, had declined. Thereafter the foremost goal of French leaders, unrealistic though it was, was to expel England from Egypt. So passionately Anglophobe had French opinion become that for Edward to schedule a visit there in the new century looked to be (in the words of one French diplomat) "a bold, not to say reckless decision." Britain's Cabinet was opposed. The risk was too great, claimed his ministers. But Edward went ahead with his visit to Paris. In the course of his dazzling state visits to the courts of Europe, Edward learned that Émile Loubet, President of France, was visiting Algeria, of which the French had taken possession in the early 1880s. Edward dispatched four battleships to salute the President. Loubet cabled his thanks and urged Edward to visit on his way back.

King Edward's state visit to Paris in the spring of 1903 was one of the turning points in the politics of the twentieth century. He told the people of Paris that he was one of their own—and they believed it. The French President caught the popular mood beforehand in the perfect phrase: "We shall always think of him," said Loubet, "as Prince of Wales."[11] The joyousness that all the world associated with France and the French at their best somehow was embodied in the Prince of Wales, who had appreciated to the full everything that France and the French had to offer.

The crowds shouted; the opinion of the country was carried; a return visit by the French President to London took place. It seems that what Edward had in mind was something more than a successful state visit. What now commenced was a process in which, after a thousand years of conflict, Britain and France became friends. What they developed was an association that was different from an alliance: it was an *entente*, a warm understanding.

To do that required reaching an agreement on *all* outstanding differences. Lord Lansdowne, as Britain's Foreign Secretary, saw the need for it; he and his colleagues supplied what was needed. The leaders of the two countries went to work and narrowed all disagreements to a half dozen; and of these, they found that the paramount conflict was over northern Africa: Egypt and Morocco. They reached a clean and simple solution. As far as England was concerned, France could have Morocco; and as far as France was concerned, England could continue to hold Egypt.

The negotiations were carried out mainly by Lord Lansdowne, Théophile Delcassé, and Paul Cambon. These men have received great credit for their roles in bringing the process to a successful conclusion.

THE ENTENTE CORDIALE was a loose arrangement between Britain and France, settling a wide range of controversies that had plagued relations between them for years. It was a bundle of agreements. It was, in a sense, both more and less than an alliance. It did not pledge the two empires to go to war together. British students of the relevant documents describe the collection of agreements as "a comprehensive, although by no means a final, settlement of Anglo-French differences in the colonial field."[12] It dealt with issues that had arisen in Europe and on the far side of the world; across oceans, and in distant continents.[13]

The agreement could be viewed, as it was by some on the Continent, as a mere liquidation of imperial conflicts: principally as the swap of Morocco for Egypt. But the words *entente cordiale*—"friendly understanding"—suggested, as Edward seems to have intended, a continuing political intimacy. When looked at in the context of a world of European alliances in which Germany and Austria-Hungary might one day fight France and Russia, it pointed to the possibility that one day Britain might also have to ally with Russia, czarist though it was. Seen through German eyes, therefore, the Anglo-French Entente of 1904 threatened encirclement; and for this Germany and its Emperor blamed the English King.

Germany, since 1882, led the Triple Alliance, which consisted, in addition to itself, of Austria-Hungary and Italy. Austria–Hungary was not entirely reliable. Italy's loyalty was even less reliable than that.

26 SHOWDOWN IN MOROCCO

In the Algeciras Conference the outline of the Great War
was already visible.

Kaiser William II, *Memoirs*[1]

THE WORLD IN WHICH the English King and the American President had taken office was haunted by its past wars and its continuing feuds.

In the maze of European international politics at the turn of the century, like Ariadne's thread, showing the way out, was France's decades-old quarrel with Germany. In the war of 1870–1871, Germany had taken possession of France's eastern province of Alsace and parts of Lorraine as well; thereafter France hoped and dreamed that the territories might be taken back.

France was no match in industrial or military strength, or in population size, for Germany. To hold its own in its long quarrel with Germany, it therefore had to enter into an alliance with some other Great Power. The power with which it was able to combine forces was Russia. So, beginning in the 1890s, France was allied with Russia.

Russia had been willing to join forces with France against Germany because Germany was opposed to Russian expansion in the Balkans, and instead, in that vast borderland between Europe and Asia, supported Austria on racial grounds: Teuton versus Slav.

When the German government received word of the Anglo-French Entente of 1904, it was not entirely sure what to make of it. As between the rival coalitions of France-Russia versus Germany-Austria, the Entente seemed to add one more player to the France-Russia side. It looked as though Great Britain might conceivably be joining France and Russia. But the timing of the news suggested something else to the head of the German government, Chancellor Bernhard von Bülow. Of the various chancellors who served under Kaiser William II, Bülow enjoyed the reputation of being the one who could get William to do what he wanted—rather than what William wanted—most often. This was such a case.

As all the political world knew, in that year (1904–1905) Russia and Japan were fighting a war that Russia was losing disastrously. Indeed, the parties to the conflict asked President Roosevelt to help negotiate a peace agreement. For doing so, he later would win the Nobel Peace Prize: the first American to be so honored.

From Bülow's point of view, the relevant fact was that in a riposte against formation of the Entente, he could move against France without worrying that France's hitherto powerful ally, Russia, would come to her aid. Indeed, he could isolate France by taking issue with it in a corner of the world where France, arguably, was in the wrong—and where (Bülow imagined) all of Europe would have to agree that such was the case. That corner of the world, as the German government saw it, was Morocco.

In 1880–1881 some of the countries of Europe had met and had made an agreement on the status and future of Morocco. They had agreed that no one of them would take an exclusive or privileged position in that country: that there would be an "open door" in Morocco, and that no European country would seek to own or dominate it either wholly or in part, and that they could trade and invest on equal terms.

Now, however, France, which governed neighboring Algeria and Tunisia, emboldened by the Entente Cordiale with England, set out to stake just such claims in Morocco. The French government acted as though the Entente agreements, which authorized it to do whatever it liked in Morocco so far as the British were concerned, authorized them to do so as far as everybody else was concerned too. In a way they were right, since they had obtained agreement from other European countries; but they had failed to consult Germany.

Soon after conclusion of the Entente Cordiale, French representatives obtained from the Sultan of Morocco a package agreement in which, among other provisions, the Sultan assented to a program of internal reform and also agreed to obtain financing only from French banks, and in which 60 percent of customs receipts would serve as collateral for loans. France had violated the 1880 treaty. Bülow saw in that a chance to isolate France.

Bülow proposed that the Kaiser should take a dramatic personal stand against French imperialism. He was to do so in the course of a cruise that William was taking in the Mediterranean Sea. The Kaiser was reluctant to agree. He had not definitely committed himself, and indeed had not done so until after his vessel, the *Hamburg*, actually arrived at the Moroccan port city of Tangier. Apparently fearing war, William also favored keeping France preoccupied with North Africa. But in the end William played the role in which his Chancellor had cast him. It was announced that he would add a stop to his cruise itinerary—Tangier, in Morocco. There was a certain symmetry in this. Edward had shaken up European politics by adding a port of call on his cruise in 1903. Now William would shake them back by adding a port of call of his own in 1905.

MARCH 31, 1905. Local notables and foreign diplomats lined up on the shore to greet the German Emperor, braving a hideous storm. Welcoming crowds shrieked. It was enough to daunt anyone. Kaiser William stood unhappy and undecided on the bridge of the *Hamburg* before finally deciding to go ahead with the landing in Tangier—in a Force 8 gale! German sailors carried him from landing craft to shore. Others lifted him onto a horse, which he apparently could not control. It was not clear what he was doing or where he was going. Members of the resident consular corps did not wait in the storm for his decision; they took shelter at the German legation, where they knew that a reception had been prepared for them. Eventually William arrived at the legation and mumbled a short speech. Nobody seems to have heard it. The next day written copies of his speech were distributed by the German legation. Their message was, in effect, anti-imperialist. He committed Germany to support the independence of Morocco.

On April 4, 1905, King Edward wrote of William to French President Loubet: "The way my nephew behaves defies description. He neither knows what he is doing or what he is after."[2]

MOROCCO WAS AN AMORPHOUS territory in northwest Africa across from Europe. The Sultan was of questionable legitimacy; and his writ did not often run. Law was rarely enforced, and crime was almost never punished. Morocco's location, however, was said to be strategic. The French wanted it because they already had Algeria and Tunisia. If they eventually absorbed Morocco, it would round off their North African empire.

Under the banners of liberation, the Kaiser's government now championed the cause of the Sultan. Bülow was not really for Morocco; he was against France.

Germany embarked on a campaign of intimidation against France, not hesitating to threaten war. French Foreign Minister Théophile Delcassé was the focal point of the attack.

Delcassé was the political heir of the republican patriotic leader Léon Gambetta, a charismatic figure to whom the Prince of Wales was greatly attracted. Starting in 1876, Bertie and Gambetta had been involved in serious discussions aimed at an English-French entente. Gambetta died on December 31, 1882; and Delcassé had picked up the fallen banner. A successful political journalist, he was appointed France's Foreign Minister in 1898.

As the most dynamic and effective proponent of France's alliances with England and Russia, who also established warm relations with the United States, he served as the target for Bülow's attack. The German government announced that it would cut off communications with the French government unless Delcassé was dismissed. Government colleagues, even those who previously had supported Delcassé, now deserted him. Edward went to the very limits of what he could do as a constitutional monarch, but could not commit his government to support the beleaguered French Foreign Minister.

On June 6, 1905, Delcassé was dismissed. The Kaiser made Bülow a prince. But the dismissal was not enough, for Berlin claimed that the Entente Cordiale itself was invalid and declared that it must be proclaimed null and void.

This was a most extraordinary demand. Britain and France had completed an agreement; Germany now claimed that it would cancel that agreement. It would rescind the Entente Cordiale. By what right would it do so? How could a pact be rescinded by someone who was not a party to it?

AT THE END OF APRIL, Edward stopped off in Paris after his own Mediterranean cruise, and met with an informal envoy from Berlin who reassured the King that it was just that Germany felt left out. The conversations misled; Edward left with the impression that the international storm would blow over—but it did not.

In early May a personal representative of the Kaiser arrived in Paris. Through a journalist trusted by both sides, the German Emperor delivered a message to the French government along roughly the following lines:

Morocco is no problem. The question is what relationship France will have with Germany. The way things are now, you act as though we do not exist. You talk to everybody else but never to us. In Paris you receive the world's leaders—except for Kaiser William. In all the great capitals of the world you are represented by distinguished ambassadors—except in Berlin, where you sent "a vacant puppet." This has got to stop. And we want to have with you not only relaxed relations but intimacy—yes, *intimacy*.

William demanded that he be awarded France's most prestigious medal, the Grand Cross of the Légion d'honneur, and he told the French government to replace its ambassador in Berlin, presumably with someone more distinguished. The message, so adolescent in its pain at being left out, was interpreted by experienced French diplomats as threatening: become intimate with us—or else we will go to war against you!

The message concluded by predicting that if France and Germany did not bind together intimately, France would ally with England. *And not at any price will we allow a Franco-British alliance.*[3]

PERHAPS THE ONLY PLACE in the world where it was believed that Germany sincerely was going to uphold the independence of Morocco was in Morocco itself. So in June 1905, now that he thought that he was free to do so, the Sultan of Morocco canceled the program of domestic reform that France had told him to enact, and renounced the French financial package that he had signed at the same time. He also invited an international congress to assemble in his homeland: in Morocco itself. Germany sponsored the plan, and may even have originated it. The conference was intended to make decisions about the future of Morocco; but from comments made by Bülow, it is clear that he had in mind a more wide-ranging discussion, particularly of Berlin's claims that it was being left out of international politics and was being encircled by the other Great Powers.

From the British and French side, and later from the American side, the great unknown was whether Germany really was prepared to go to war. Bülow believed that he would not need to do so, but nobody knows how far he might have gone if he were carried away while running a bluff.

Alfred von Schlieffen, head of the German Great General Staff, thought 1905 the ideal time to launch a preventive war against Russia and France. He may not have been alone in this. However, there were powerful interests and forces within Germany that would militate against launching an attack if Germany itself had not been attacked. William moved to dismiss and replace Schlieffen. Evidence suggests that it was because neither the Kaiser nor the Chancellor wanted a war, at least at that time.

The Kaiser, though changeable as always in his views, wrote to Bülow late in 1905 in terms that could have come out of *Alice in Wonderland*. He did not want a war, he said, until he had concluded a formal alliance with the Ottoman Empire and, indeed, with all Arabian and Moorish rulers. Nor did he want a war in 1906, when the army would be renewing artillery. "But the greatest obstacle to a war is that we could not take a single man out of the country because of the Socialist menace—Shoot down the Socialists first, behead them, put them out of action, if necessary massacre the lot—and then war abroad! But not before."[4]

GERMANY HAD CHOSEN Tangier—a Moroccan city—as the site for the conference. It then became known that the city's chief was al-Raisuni, the notorious criminal made famous by the Roosevelt administration at the Republican National Convention of 1904: "Perdicaris alive or Raisuni dead!"[5] Douglas Porch, the author of *The Conquest of Morocco*, entertains the notion of what might have happened if the world's leading diplomats had assembled as guests of a professional kidnapper.[6] Because of Raisuni, and to the disappointment of the Germans, therefore, the site of the proposed international conference had to be moved. Eventually it was convened, not in Morocco itself, but in the Reina Cristina hotel in Algeciras in southern Spain.

. . .

BUT FRANCE WOULD NOT agree to the holding of the conference. The Great Powers were deadlocked, France versus Germany. Did it mean war?

In his memoirs, written years later, Bülow maintained that from the start there had been "a difference of opinion between the Kaiser and myself. In His Majesty's opinion it was in Germany's best interests for France to commit and engage herself in Morocco. This would turn the eyes of Frenchmen away [from Alsace-Lorraine]."[7]

But Bülow doubted that *anything* would turn their eyes away from Alsace-Lorraine. The Chancellor claimed that "for some-time past I had been keeping my eye on Morocco, fully aware of a possible, even closer *rapprochement* between France and England, through the exchange of Morocco for Egypt."[8] The Entente was a recent and untried creation; why not smash it at birth by driving a wedge between the British and French empires?

27 | ON TO ALGECIRAS

THEODORE ROOSEVELT was a man of secrets. From his earliest days in politics, he had recognized that he (and Lodge) were a minority of two: that if he were to openly avow his true beliefs, he would be voted down by the electorate or defeated in the Congress or blocked by key officials. So it was as he set out to outplay Kaiser William in the great game of international politics that was about to unfold in Morocco. It was typical that TR allowed the Kaiser to imagine that he had TR's support.

In carrying out the negotiations that were about to begin, Roosevelt confided, among only a few others, in Secretary of State Root, U.S. Ambassador to Italy Henry White (who served as U.S. delegate to Algeciras), U.S. Ambassador to Great Britain Whitelaw Reid, and, to some extent, the German and French ambassadors to the United States.

Jean Jules Jusserand was the French Ambassador to the United States. He was TR's favorite ambassador. When European affairs were in question, Roosevelt would almost always turn to him. Among other things, Jusserand was fair-minded; could see when his country was in the wrong; and was prepared to compromise in order to keep the peace.

Berlin's man in Washington was in a quite similar position, and enjoyed nearly as favored a relationship with the American President.

On March 6, 1905, and again on March 7, Hermann Speck von Sternburg, the German Ambassador, came to speak to Roosevelt about the Kaiser's diplomatic venture in Morocco. Washington had employed considerable pressure on Berlin to get Sternburg appointed to be Ambassador to the United States.

On March 6 and March 7 the German Ambassador brought messages from the Kaiser. They can best be understood in the light of the evidence we have that William II hero-worshipped Roosevelt. According to Bülow,

> Theodore Roosevelt, the President of the United States, exercised a quite particular fascination over the Kaiser. "That's my man!" he used to say, as soon as the name of Roosevelt was mentioned. He read in dispatches from our ambassador that Roosevelt performed feats of riding equal to those of a cowboy, that, like Buffalo Bill, he could just hit the bull's eye with deadly marksmanship at a prodigious distance, that his spirit was unquenchable, fearless, and ready for anything.[1]

What Sternburg was directed to ask was whether Roosevelt would join William in telling the Sultan of Morocco that their two countries would uphold an open-door regime in Morocco. Such a regime would aim at keeping any one of the Great Powers from establishing a privileged position: a position enabling them to exercise exclusive control over Morocco. Those powers trying to seize exclusive control were France, primarily, and Spain.

Germany had a strong case. France had been in the process of penetrating and absorbing Morocco for decades. Berlin was not wrong in believing that French expansion in that territory would continue for decades more.[2]

Nor were the Germans wrong in believing that in the treaty of 1880–1881, France had promised to Europe and the United States not to exclude any of them, but in fact was doing so.

Had the Morocco crisis that Germany was precipitating really been about Morocco, King Edward and President Roosevelt might have reacted differently than they did. But it was not about Morocco; it was about the Entente Cordiale.

Roosevelt replied, assuring Germany of America's warmest friendship and hopes for world peace; but saying that the United States did not have significant interests in Morocco, as would justify becoming involved in that country's affairs.

TR reminded Speck that America was an isolationist country, unwilling to involve itself in global affairs; and that the Congress had given him many difficulties even in regard to his participation in Western Hemisphere affairs. "Should I now engage myself in Morocco, a land which is here entirely unknown . . . I would expose myself to the bitterest attacks."[3] If he took one step in Moroccan affairs, he continued, he would have to be prepared to take more; but, he said, in an important statement of his policy, he would take no step at all in foreign policy "if I am not certain that eventually I can carry out my intentions with force."[4]

The following month William replied that he now had news that England had agreed to back the French-Spanish combine. Italy, he said, had raised the possibility that Britain's backing might be by force of arms. William then claimed that England's attitude would depend on that of the United States; so (William asked) would Roosevelt please tell London that the United States agreed that there should be a conference? Otherwise Germany would have to consider making war on France.

Roosevelt was bear-hunting in Colorado at the time. But he kept William Howard Taft, his Acting President, fully informed. He regarded the Kaiser's rantings as a "pipe-dream." His view was that the United States should stay out of the matter. "I do not feel that as a Government we should interfere in the Morocco matter. We have other fish to fry and we have no real interest in Morocco. I do not care to take sides between France and Germany in the matter."

Roosevelt deplored the conflict between Britain and Germany at this time. He regarded their fears of each other as, in many cases, unfounded. In the long run, he conceived of Germany as the leading threat to the United States, to the United Kingdom, to the European balance of power, and to the peace of the world. But to Henry White, his favorite American diplomat, he wrote in the summer of 1905, "I want to keep on good terms with Germany, and if possible to prevent a rupture between Germany and France. But my sympathies have at bottom been with France and I suppose will continue so . . ."[5]

On his return to Washington, Roosevelt found Speck and Jusserand, two of his closest friends, seriously worried that war might break out between their countries and might even spread into a worldwide "conflagration." Their concern communicated itself to the President; and at last he agreed to intervene. TR's America, isolationist as it was, intended to keep the peace in Europe.

Roosevelt put all of his prestige on the line. Through Jusserand, he asked the French government to reverse its position and agree to the conference. In fact, as scholars have discovered only recently, France already had decided to do so. But in replying to Roosevelt, the French government claimed that it was only because of its esteem for the American President that it was willing to agree. In turn, in communicating with Berlin, Roosevelt gave all credit to Kaiser William. He claimed that it was due to William's outstanding diplomacy that this hitherto seemingly impossible result had been achieved.

Throughout the negotiations his consistent practice with William was to lay on the flattery with a trowel. He called the French cave-in on the conference "a diplomatic triumph of the first magnitude" and "a genuine triumph"; and he called William "the leader among the sovereigns of to-day." At the same time he urged the Kaiser to be magnanimous in victory, and not to haggle over minor issues which would cloud Germany's victory.

ONE OF THE ARGUMENTS that TR used in persuading the French government to agree to a conference was that, if Germany started a war against France at that time, Germany would win it. Germany was a land power, and its troops would swiftly sweep over France. Britain, a naval power, would be powerless to help; by the time it was ready to do something, the war would be over long since. It went without saying that France's ally, Russia, was still *hors de combat* from its defeat by Japan.

This argument struck home. It inspired the Entente countries to take precautions for the future. The new British Foreign Secretary, Sir Edward Grey, authorized secret staff talks to begin between British and French military leaders. These paved the way for a British

Expeditionary Force to participate in the opening day of the First World War on the continent of Europe a decade later. This may well have been the outstanding achievement of the conference.

IN PREPARING FOR THE conference, Roosevelt was aware of having an ace up his sleeve. Speck had transmitted from Berlin a personal message in which the Kaiser pledged, should the conference deadlock, that Germany would abide by whatever terms Roosevelt regarded as "most practical and fair." TR was skeptical. He remarked later that "as my experience has always been that a promise needlessly entered into is rarely kept, I never expected the Kaiser to keep this one, and he has not."[6]

28 | HIGH NOON

ALGECIRAS IS A FISHING port in the south of Spain, some six miles west of Gibraltar. It lies across the straits from Morocco, where the Middle East begins. Its mild climate made it a winter resort town long ago; and it remains a resort town today.

In attendance were representatives of the United States, the United Kingdom, and the several states of Europe that then had a voice in international affairs.

The conference, convened at the request of the Sultan of Morocco, was sponsored by Germany. Invitations were sent out in 1905. The conference was scheduled for January 1906.

The ostensible purpose of the meeting was to discuss the future of Morocco. At the time, Morocco was a territory of uncertain boundaries, with few resources and only the phantom of a government. Though it could well have used a coherent plan for its future, that was not the real goal of the Algeciras Conference.

The real goal of the meeting was to sort out the future, not of Morocco, but of Europe. William II had called the conference in

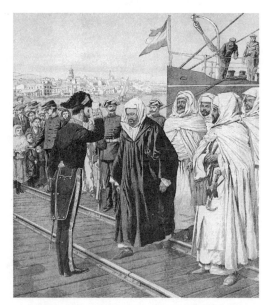

*The Moroccan delegation arrives at Algeciras for
negotiations, 1906.*

order to challenge the existing alignment of European states: an
alignment in which the British Empire, France, and Russia had begun
to stand against Germany. Later this alignment would carry over into
the First World War.

The Algeciras Conference convened January 16, 1906, and adjourned three months later.

From Algeciras, one could see the coast of Morocco across the
water. Having established themselves in their own villas, the delegates of France, the United Kingdom, and Morocco put themselves
at ease. The other delegates were accommodated at the Hotel Reina
Cristina, the traditional best hotel in town. Each delegation had its
own table, flying its own flag, in the dining room. Eavesdropping
must have been rife.

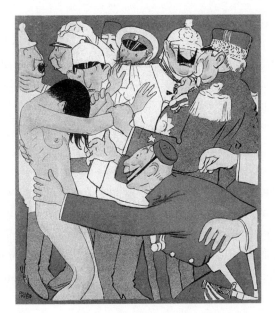

A 1906 French cartoon depicting the European powers' struggle over Morocco.

Most newspaper correspondents checked in at the Hotel Anglo-Hispano; it was said to be a journalist's paradise. Those who expected little in the way of entertainment brought their own: a secretary in the Russian delegation brought along his violin; a reporter burst out in Neapolitan songs.

The conference hall was a half mile away from the Reina Cristina. Negotiations apparently were conducted mostly in hotel rooms; and White, the U.S. delegate, could be seen shuttling among suites. In such an atmosphere, it was difficult to keep secrets or to separate lies from truth. Rumors were launched in the morning, spread during the day, and officially denied in the evening: such was the picture painted by André Tardieu, a French journalist, foreign editor of *Le Temps*, and future Prime Minister.

.   .   .

THERE WAS A NONOFFICIAL observer at the Algeciras conference. In addition to the official British delegate, Sir Donald MacKenzie Wallace, though accredited by the London *Times*, attended sessions as the personal representative of King Edward. He was a trusted confidant. His presence indicated that, though it was TR who was making the play, Edward felt deeply involved.

Edward's man Wallace was in attendance as the King's watchdog to make sure that Britain fully supported France; and Wallace may have been the spokesman for Edward who told French ambassador Paul Cambon or had an envoy tell him: "Tell us what you wish on each point and we will support you without restriction or reserves."[1]

In its origin, in the brain of German Chancellor von Bülow, the Morocco crisis that was meant to be resolved at the conference aimed at dividing Britain from France, and at rallying other European countries against France. It accomplished neither goal.

Bülow seems to have hoped that Britain would desert France in a time of danger, for the two empires had been rivals for so long and still coveted many of the same overseas territories. Instead, Germany's threats drew the two countries together.

The German government seemed surprised that it received so little support at Algeciras from other European countries at the conference, such as Spain, Italy, and Russia. France had reached private agreements with Spain (for a participation in whatever France got in Morocco) and Italy (France would not object when Italy moved to take Libya). Russia depended on French financing and therefore had to vote for France. By March 1906 the German delegate in Algeciras cabled Berlin that, for one reason or another, "all powers but Austria were lined up against Germany."[2] Crisis loomed on all sides, as the British delegate, Sir Arthur Nicolson, supposedly proposed to break up the conference—within a matter of days. The chief German delegate called for Roosevelt to mediate and thus save the conference.

On March 7, 1906, TR cabled William proposing compromise terms, essentially favorable to France, that (as he explained) were, in his view, fair and practical—reminding the Kaiser of his earlier promise to accept whatever terms TR found fair and practical. Germany counter-offered. The President took this as the Kaiser breaking his word. TR threatened to make public the entire record; and when the Germans surrendered, he believed that it was this threat that brought about the surrender. Only twenty years later was it learned

The Conference of Algeciras, 1906.

that the so-called pledge was a misunderstanding. Speck, Germany's ambassador, had either misunderstood or exceeded his instructions. The pledge was from the Chancellor (not the Kaiser) and it promised to recommend (not accept) TR's terms. Having learned from the files that the pledge had been made, the German government honored it. It was widely considered to be a German retreat.

IN THE RECRIMINATIONS THAT broke out in Germany after the 1914 war, the Kaiser and his entourage blamed the war on the English "policy of encirclement" undertaken in the Algeciras Conference. The Kaiser, in the memoirs that appeared under his name decades later, claimed that "the pro-French and anti-German attitude of England, which there came out into the open, was due to special orders from King Edward VII, who had sent Sir D. MacKenzie Wallace to Algeciras as his 'supervising representative' equipped with personal instructions."[3] According to the Kaiser, Wallace later gave hints to his friends that his instructions were to be pro-France and anti-Germany.

KAISER WILHELM NEVER guessed that Roosevelt and Edward were working together. The secret was kept. The King had remained in the background, and had let the President manage things on behalf of both of them. It had worked.

TR was proud of his achievement. In a confidential letter to Edward dated April 25, 1906, he invited praise. "I think the outcome of the Morocco business was satisfactory, don't you?" he wrote. At the same time he hinted at tales that could not yet be told; he suggested that "I had some amusing experiences in the course of the negotiations"—without revealing what they were.[4]

The conference adjourned in April 1906. The necessary signatures in time were obtained on the Act of Algeciras, the treaty that concluded matters. In the event, the French got everything they wanted; the alliance with Britain held; joint staff talks between the French and British military were initiated, and proved to be more binding than any signatures; and the United States made an appearance on the world stage.

TO SOFTEN THE BLOW of Algeciras, King Edward, along with Charles Hardinge, met with Kaiser William and other German leaders. The Britons explained to the Germans that they had to negotiate an entente with France because they had differences with France. Since they had no specific differences with Germany—only rivalries!—there was no need to sign any agreements with Berlin.

"THE CONFERENCE OF Algeciras was a decisive moment in European diplomacy," the British historian A. J. P. Taylor was to write decades later. "With uncanny foreboding, it anticipated the course of policy which the Great Powers would follow even when diplomacy gave way to war. It was the first great demonstration of the Triple Entente; it was the first demonstration, too, that Italy was drifting away from the Triple Alliance and that the United States [was] drifting into sympathy with the *Entente Cordiale*. The conference was more than a demonstration of alliances and friendships; it helped to create them. When the delegates went to Algeciras, relationships between the Powers still seemed fluid; when the conference ended, a pattern of European affairs was laid down which lasted . . . until the end of the First World War."[5]

The Moroccan crisis had set the nations of the world on the road to war.

29 WHO MOVES HISTORY?

THE OPENING YEARS OF THE twentieth century proved to be an era of transition in British as well as world politics. Tories continued to govern, but not the same Tories as in the 1890s, and not in pursuit of the same agenda. Salisbury, who preached "splendid isolation," had been replaced by Prime Minister Balfour and Foreign Secretary Lansdowne: internationalists, who sought friendship with the other Great Powers. Then a split within the Tories drove them to call new elections—which they lost. Taking office, the Liberal Prime Minister Sir Henry Campbell-Bannerman (1905–1908) and the Liberal Foreign Secretary Sir Edward Grey (1905–1916) were statesmen whom King Edward and President Roosevelt found congenial. Working with Grey, Roosevelt at last was enabled to persuade London to send sympathetic envoys to Washington—and then to resolve all remaining conflicts between the United States and the United Kingdom.

Not merely did Britain have a new Foreign Secretary; it had a changed Foreign Office. As holdovers from the long reign of Lord

Salisbury left office, replacements sponsored by King Edward took their place, and the new men reorganized the institution. Formerly, even senior officials left policy formation to the Foreign Secretary. Now even quite junior officials advised their chiefs on policy matters. They believed, as Edward did, in an alliance with France and Russia to defend against Germany.

At the time of the Algeciras Conference, Grey resisted pressure from Francis Bertie and Louis Mallet, strongly anti-German officials, to ally with France.

Francis Bertie was British ambassador to France. Mallet was Grey's private secretary. Grey explained that British public opinion, parliamentary public opinion, and even opinion within the governing Liberal Party would strongly oppose contracting an alliance that would commit Britain to go to war.

Instead, Grey authorized unofficial talks between the War Office of the United Kingdom and the French Military Attaché as to how the armed forces of Britain and France could collaborate in the event of a war against Germany. These were the talks that grew out of the Morocco crisis.

A further meeting convened the following year between the British army and the British navy, at which officials recommended that in the event of war one hundred thousand British troops should be sent to France.

It was a characteristic of the diplomacy of Grey that he did not inform most of his Cabinet colleagues what he had done. Like Roosevelt, he believed that if others knew what he was doing or planning to do, they would disapprove and might try to stop him. Later—after August 1914—a number of antiwar critics were to blame the outbreak of the World War on his secret commitments.

. . .

CHANGING THE COURSE of the ship of state—Britain's world policy—from what it had been in the eighteenth century to what it would be in the twentieth century was somewhat like turning a battleship around to go in the opposite direction. It was done slowly. In the case of world policy, it took years.

From 1900, when Britain considered ending its isolation, through 1901, when it considered allying with Germany, to 1902, when it briefly allied with Japan, to 1903, when Edward won over the Parisians, to 1904, when the Entente Cordiale was concluded, to the Morocco crisis of 1905–1906, when the United States and Britain acted as secret allies to defend the Entente Cordiale, it took until 1907, when Britain and Russia settled their differences, to wind things up.

Fittingly it was on January 1, 1907, that Britain's new policy received its classic exposition. It was in a memorandum submitted by the Foreign Office official Eyre Crowe. Crowe was one of the chief architects of the new Foreign Office. Born in Germany, he was educated in Germany and France. He was someone of overwhelming erudition. The author Harold Nicolson described him in a range of splendid adjectives: "industrious, loyal, expert, accurate, beloved, obedient, and courageous."[1]

Crowe began his memorandum by reviewing recent history. He pictured the Morocco crisis as an attempt to break up the Entente Cordiale. Berlin, he said, would view the Entente as an alliance directed against Germany, even though it wasn't that. Berlin would see it that way because Bismarck's policy was to encourage all other European countries to quarrel with one another.

Crowe pictured the European situation in balance-of-power terms. As an island country, Britain's interest was in keeping any one hegemon from becoming preponderant on the Continent. It was in keeping all states independent. Germany—consciously or not—was engaged in a drive for dominance in Europe. Maybe it did not realize that it was doing so, but that was what it was doing nonetheless. Its geopolitical situation compelled it to do so.

BRITAIN'S EVENTUAL TURNABOUT in world affairs was so momentous an event that many claimed the credit for it. Looking back,

King Edward VII, with his nephew, Kaiser Wilhelm of Germany, photographed together at an unknown official occasion in 1905.

Arthur Balfour and Sir Edward Grey (Viscount Grey of Fallodon, as he became) claimed that King Edward had nothing to do with the Entente Cordiale or with the turn against Germany.

George Monger, a leading student of these events, agrees. He writes that "the King had almost no influence on the formation of policy, and his own views were too personal and impulsive for him to be a successful diplomat."[2]

"He never showed understanding of the larger, impersonal forces bearing upon the relations between states."[3] Moreover, "his concern for personalities rather than facts and his own formidable personality made him a powerful ally for those he favored . . . "[4] But Monger admits that "every action of his was important; for the world was still ruled monarchically."[5]

That may well be the point that historians sometimes miss: Edward did not make the agreements with the Allies and the United States; but it was because of Edward that the agreements were made.

ROOSEVELT AND EDWARD held similar worldviews. Both believed that the best way to keep the peace was to build up armed strength to deter potential aggressors. Both identified Germany and Japan as the chief dangers to their countries—and Russia too, further down the road. Both were pro-French.

Since the 1890s, France had held off Germany by allying with Russia. Now that the English-French alliance was in effect, France wanted to bring Russia into contact with Britain too. The British Foreign Office already was considering how to resolve the outstanding conflicts between the two countries, almost all of which were in Asia.

King Edward had been in favor of an association with Russia all along. The problem was that the Russian government was distasteful. The Czar's domains were notorious for pogroms and injustice.

Edward worried that if he proposed a Russian alliance—and if the proposal were rejected—he would never have another chance to get the proposal accepted. So timing would be everything. In choosing his moment, he relied heavily on Sir Donald MacKenzie Wallace, Britain's outstanding expert on Russia.

On August 31, 1907, Britain's conflicts with Russia were resolved. The "Great Game" that had pitted Britain against France and Russia ever since Napoleon's time was over. London had opted to protect its interests in Europe rather than its empire abroad. Dimly ahead, the leaders of the North Atlantic democracies could see that in the twentieth century they would repel Germany with Russia's help and then Russia with Germany's help. The new age of President Roosevelt and King Edward had begun.

FRIEDRICH VON HOLSTEIN, the dominant figure in the German Foreign Office in its post-Bismarck years, did not believe—as the Kaiser did—that King Edward was responsible for the close relationship that had developed between France and England. The King's actions, in his view, although not "very friendly . . . with regard to Germany," were "not likely to change the groupings of the powers, which is dictated by force of circumstances *and not by the contributions of statesmen.*"[6]

Why the reversal of Great Power alliances occurred at the turn of the century can be debated endlessly. It did not have to happen; nor, if it did happen, did it have to happen in that way. Germany could have given up the naval race against England, for example, and could have accepted the offer of alliance held out by Chamberlain. If so, the other power constellations could have been expected to fall into place in such a way as to take account of these new realities.

It should go without saying that the revolution that took place in and around the 1900s, which stood the structure of international politics on its head, was not the work of President Roosevelt and King Edward alone. It can be argued, and usually is, that such cataclysmic shiftings of the political tectonic plates are the workings of vast, impersonal, and complex forces. It also was the result of contributions by many others. There are those who plausibly argue that the change of alliances, with all its consequences, would have taken place even if King Edward and President Roosevelt had never been born. That seems doubtful. France would not have entered into the Entente Cordiale if the King had not personally persuaded France to do so; and it is entirely possible that the Kaiser would not have backed down at Algeciras if President Roosevelt had not been involved. There also is a strong case for crediting both the American and the Englishman for having made a start—even if it was *only* a start—in pulling their respective countries out of their deep-rooted isolationism in foreign policy.

Certainly personalities played a great role in the decision making of the leaders on all sides. Germany forced the French to fire their Foreign Secretary Théophile Delcassé; it was a principal goal of their foreign policy. And Kaiser William first pictured the Algeciras Conference, and therefore the First World War to which it seemingly led, as a personal duel between himself and his uncle Edward VII: a mano a mano in that small Spanish town. Indeed, ever since Edward's accession to the throne in 1901, William had seen his lifelong hatred for his uncle the King as moving toward some sort of climax. In the end—as he saw it—modern history would be the story of their showdown.

William's fatal error was in believing that it was going to be only two of them shooting it out in Algeciras. As it turned out, there were three.

THE 1900S WERE AN AGE of reversals, in which enemies became friends and friends became enemies. After three decades of peace among the Great Powers, war once again was openly discussed in the capital cities of Europe.

In this time of new dangers, new opportunities, and new possibilities, as traditional allegiances and alliances were questioned, Edward and Theodore saw that the American national interest and the British national interest had become identical. The two countries were no longer rivals, as they had been for more than a century. England's new monarch and America's new President, both of them liberal imperialists, shared a belief that it would be best for the world if the English-speaking peoples were to dominate it.

As both men saw it, the new danger that had arisen in the international politics of their time was the threat to the European balance of power posed by German militarism under Kaiser William II. Their shared goal was to restrain Germany; and that also meant protecting France.

At Algeciras, the Western powers won. But it was only the first round of a conflict that brought about two world wars and a cold war that did not come to an end until the last Russian soldier left German soil on August 31, 1994.

Where a country took its place in the world was determined by its relative power: that was the view of President Roosevelt, who could not, however, avow it, because it was not at all the view of his countrymen. Roosevelt's faith was that of the English-speaking peoples, whose cause was righteousness; but that was his faith only after the Boer War persuaded him that England could no longer do America any harm. His object was to be on top and to keep the peace by preparing for war. His policy was to preserve the world balance of power by supporting those countries that were on the way down, and therefore posed no threat—England and France—as against those, such as Germany and Japan, that were dangerously on the way up.

But once power considerations had determined which side he would choose to support, he would of course be able to justify his decision on ideological grounds. That is something that politicians learn to do.

Roosevelt's almost mechanistic realism—his apparent view that power determines a country's policy—is one that echoes today, and presumably will continue to do so: it can be persuasive.

IN TASTES AND HABITS, few men could have been more unlike each other than the two leaders of the English-speaking world in the Edwardian age. Both, it is true, were to an extent self-invented: Roosevelt as a Westerner, Wales as a Frenchman. One had been accused of being a prig; the other was a confirmed philanderer. Roosevelt was not a mannerless savage; Edward was not a mindless playboy.

Edward's politics were personal. Those of his adversaries were too. Kaiser William viewed the run-up to the First World War as a duel between his uncle and himself. Edward made an effort to keep it from becoming that. Even though their family conflict did not cause the war, it appears to have had an effect on events, at least in a sense.

If instead of fighting, the two men had become friends, working together to straighten out misunderstandings, it might have had a positive effect. Presidents were not the only decision makers in the early 1900s; the actions of monarchs still had an impact in those days.

AS THE MOROCCO crisis of 1905–1906 demonstrated, the President and the King, though coming from different directions, tended to come out at the same place.

In 1905, when the crisis began, Roosevelt was afraid that Germany was going to launch a war against France. The President had come to oppose war. In addition he was afraid of what might happen in this particular war. He was certain that Germany would quickly invade, defeat, and occupy France. France would lose its independence and become a satellite of Germany's. That would overthrow the existing balance of power in Europe. Disorder would follow. So Germany had to be stopped.

Considerations of power certainly moved the British Foreign Office, as well, to champion an alliance with France. But everything that we know about Edward, as Prince of Wales and as King, suggests that such objective circumstances were not his chief concern. In this he was like a prince from some other age, ruled as much by heart as by head. It looks very much as though he took France's side in the world quarrels of the twentieth century for the simplest of reasons: it was because he loved France. It was because France made him happy and made the world happy. This may not sound like a serious reason—but it was probably the true one.

30 | TIME RUNS OUT

THEODORE ROOSEVELT HAD pledged not to run again for President in 1908. But his six years in office flew by swiftly. At home they had been turbulent, tumultuous years. Not only in domestic politics, but even in foreign affairs, which were relatively calm, he had only just begun. He kept his Algeciras papers secret, even though opponents in the Senate demanded to see them; but the basic issue of what role the United States should play in world affairs remained for future generations to decide.[1]

For Edward the King the countdowns began early. The cigars and rich foods and late nights took their toll. By about 1906 his deterioration started to become visible.

EDWARD DIED SUDDENLY in the spring of 1910. His death marked the end of an era. The royalty of seventy nations gathered at his funeral. They came to say farewell to Edward; but, as it turned out, they said farewell to themselves: it was "the greatest assemblage of

King Edward VII's funeral procession, May 1910.

royalty and rank ever gathered in one place," Barbara Tuchman remarked, "and, of its kind, the last."[2] Monarchy was about to be swept away in the wars of the twentieth century. It was last seen on full parade at Edward's funeral.

Heading the procession was Edward's riderless charger, its saddle empty, accompanied only by Edward's terrier Caesar.

On that bright May day, nine kings rode on horseback through the palace gates, three by three, "with plumed helmets, gold braid, crimson sashes, and jeweled orders flashing in the sun."[3] Their colors were scarlet, blue, green, and purple. They were followed by "five heirs apparent, forty more imperial or royal highnesses, seven queens"[4] . . . and other characters out of storybooks.

Eyes focused on the dark emperor of the north, William II, wearing the scarlet uniform of a British Field Marshal, and mounted on a gray charger.

Oddly, it was a uniform and a rank to which he was entitled. Such matters were within the province of Paul Cambon, French ambassador at the Court of St. James's, and doyen of the diplomatic corps. It was Cambon's task to notice that a proposed medal or dress or uniform was improper and must not be worn. Only Edward himself could have done the job better: since childhood he had taken a strong interest in clothes and had been a stickler for wearing the proper dress. Supposedly, Cambon too, who was vastly experienced, had seen almost everything in the way of inappropriate uniform. But nothing had prepared him for the proposal received from the official American representative at the funeral, former President Theodore Roosevelt. The former deputy sheriff from the Western badlands told Cambon that he would ride through the palace gates mounted on horseback, "dressed in khaki and boots with a Buffalo Bill hat"[5] and armed with a saber and pistols.

If there is an afterlife, Edward, looking down, must have burst into laughter.

31 | THE ROAD TO SARAJEVO

IN 1911, THE YEAR AFTER Edward died, France took military action in Morocco that violated the provisions of the Act of Algeciras. French troops marched on Fez, the seat of government, supposedly in order to rescue Europeans and to restore order. Once again, Paris had broken its word in the colonial world; and Berlin had seized the occasion to try to rally the other powers of Europe against France.

Germany dispatched a gunboat, the *Panther*, allegedly to protect Germans in Agadir, a Moroccan port on the Atlantic coast. But there were no Germans in Agadir; and the *Panther* had to wait for several days in port until a German arrived to be rescued. The international crisis that ensued was in some respects a replay of the Algeciras affair. Once again, Germany intended to drive a wedge between its European enemies; and—once again—drove them together instead. In Algeciras, Germany found itself backed only by Austria-Hungary; in Agadir, the Germans found that even the support of Austria-Hungary was heavily qualified. The German Chancellor told the

Kaiser: "If it comes to a war, we must hope that Austria is attacked so that she needs our help and not that we are attacked so that it would depend on Austria's decision whether she will remain faithful to the alliance."[1]

IN QUEEN VICTORIA'S DAY, international politics was a matter of coalitions. What we now can see is that in the Edwardian age that began to change. Germany found itself practically isolated; aggrieved, it charged that it was being encircled by its enemies, and it blamed this on King Edward and the conference of Algeciras.

The English-speaking world was moving in the opposite direction. However fitfully, Britain and the United States started to move out of, rather than into, isolation. In the decades that followed Algeciras they, along with other democracies, often chose a policy of alliances.

The Moroccan crises proved to be stepping stones on the path that led to the outbreak of the First World War in 1914—and beyond, to the 1939–1945 World War, and to the cold war that followed it. So, at least in part, President Roosevelt and King Edward, as partners, wrote the script of the twentieth century.

APPENDIX

THE ANGLO-FRENCH ENTENTE

"The agreement was signed on April 8, 1904. It was a comprehensive, although by no means a final, settlement of Anglo-French differences in the colonial field. It consisted of two conventions, the first dealing with Newfoundland and West and Central Africa, and the second with Siam, Madagascar, and the New Hebrides. Finally there was a declaration about Morocco, and five secret articles. France abandoned her pressure for England's withdrawal from Egypt and pledged her support for changes in the Egyptian financial regime. In return for this belated recognition of British predominance in Egypt, England recognized the right of France to preserve order in Morocco, and to assist the Sultan in reforming his administration and economy. The open door was to be maintained in both Egypt and Morocco for thirty years. France promised to reach agreement with Spain respecting Spanish interests in Morocco, and agreed not to erect fortifications on the Moorish coast opposite Gibraltar. The secret articles alluded to the possibility of the modification of the status quo by the two countries in Egypt and Morocco, assigned the Melilla coast to Spain in that event, and referred to the possibility of the abolition of the capitulations in Egypt and Morocco."[1]

ACKNOWLEDGMENTS

I am most grateful to Ariane Fasquelle, my French publisher at Grasset, for suggesting that I write about some aspect of the Entente Cordiale. It would never have occurred to me on my own, and it provided the germ of the idea for this book. My thanks to Ariane.

As always in any project that calls for me to put pen to paper, my wonderful agent, Suzanne Gluck at the William Morris Agency, immediately took charge, made all necessary decisions, and supplied direction. My gratitude to Suzanne, the always indispensable.

At Penguin Press, publishers of this book, my editor is Ann Godoff. She has proved to be a Maxwell Perkins—to my astonishment, for I hadn't known there was another one. My thanks to Ann for making the editing and publishing of this book such a happy experience.

Ann's assistant, Lindsay Whalen, ever-cheerful, ever-helpful, ever-knowledgeable, saw the project through with exemplary efficiency. She is a gem.

I have never before been able to use a research assistant. For once—in this book—I was able to do so: someone who has made much less work for me rather than more. Tara Isabella Burton, who had just emerged from writing a book of her own, undertook to read through some of Theodore Roosevelt's voluminous writings about himself and to select those I would want to read myself. She did an inspired job, which bodes well for the many future books of her own.

As always my old comrade in arms Robert L. Sigmon in London rushed books to me as I needed them in my travels throughout Europe. Many thanks to him.

My thanks to Louis Soubrier for showing me the love seat referred to on page 69 and Bruce Newman for having called my attention to it in the first place.

Profound thanks to Professor Kathleen Dalton, author of the leading one-volume biography of Theodore Roosevelt, and to Mr. Hugh Fremantle, a luminary of the Anglo-American literary world, for having read the book in manuscript: a chore indeed. I hope that it needs no saying that the book's shortcomings and errors are mine, not theirs.

It remains for me to express truly great gratitude to Carol Shookhoff, an alchemist, who converts my illegible longhand and ink-blots into a readable manuscript, cheerfully editing it and copyediting it as she goes along. I don't know how she does it.

New York City

NOTES

CHAPTER 1

1. Cecil Woodham-Smith, *Queen Victoria* (New York: Knopf, 1972), p. 32.
2. Elizabeth Longford, *Queen Victoria* (Thrupp, Stroud, Gloucestershire, Eng.: Sutton, 2005), p. 2.
3. Ibid., p. 4.
4. John Van der Kiste, *Queen Victoria's Children* (Thrupp, Stroud, Gloucestershire, Eng.: Sutton, 2003), p. 6.
5. Ibid., p. 11.
6. Ibid., p. 12.
7. Ibid., p. 13.
8. Longford, *Queen Victoria*, p. 50.

CHAPTER 2

1. Longford, *Queen Victoria*, p. 3.
2. All figures cited in this paragraph are from Paul M. Kennedy, *The Rise of the Anglo-German Antagonism 1860–1914*. (London: George Allen & Unwin, 1980), p. 5.

CHAPTER 3

1. Victoria's own words. Stanley Weintraub, *The Importance of Being Edward: King in Waiting 1841–1901* (London: John Murray, 2000) p. 3.
2. Keith Middlemas, *The Life and Times of Edward VII* (Garden City, N.Y.: Doubleday, 1972), p. 12.
3. Van der Kiste, *Queen Victoria's Children*, p. 17, citing Corti.
4. *The British Empire throughout the World, 1905* (Moretonhampstead, Devon: Old House Books, Sutton Mead, 1904).

5. Giles St. Aubyn, *Edward VII: Prince and King* (New York: Atheneum, 1979) p. 22.

6. Ibid.

7. Ibid., p. 22.

CHAPTER 4

1. St. Aubyn, *Edward VII*, Chapter 5.

2. Ibid., p. 19.

3. Ibid.

4. Ibid.

5. Ibid.

6. Weintraub, *Importance of Being Edward*, p. 7.

7. Ibid., p. 3.

8. St. Aubyn, *Edward VII*, pp. 22–23.

9. Weintraub, *Importance of Being Edward*, p. 15.

10. Ibid., p. 17.

11. Ian Dunlop, *Edward VII and the Entente Cordiale* (London: Constable, 2004), p. 30.

12. Weintraub, *Importance of Being Edward*, p. 36.

13. Ibid., p. 37.

CHAPTER 5

1. Gordon Brook-Shepherd, *Uncle of Europe: The Social and Diplomatic Life of Edward VII* (New York and London: Harcourt Brace Jovanovich, 1975), p. 27.

CHAPTER 6

1. *The New York Times,* "From Canada: Preparations for the Visit of H.R.H. The Prince of Wales," July 16, 1860.

2. *The New York Times,* "The Prince of Wales at Halifax," datelined July 30, 1860, published July 31, 1860.

3. *The New York Times,* "The Prince of Wales at Halifax," datelined August 1, 1860, published August 2, 1860.

4. *The New York Times,* "The Prince of Wales: His Quebec Reception and Attendant Ceremonies," August 23, 1860.

5. *The New York Times*, "Movements of the Prince," datelined September 29, 1860, published October 1, 1860.

6. Kinahan Cornwallis, *Royalty in the New World—or—The Prince of Wales in America* (New York: Doolard, 1860), p. 188.

7. Ibid., p. 213.

8. Ibid, p. 214.

9. *The New York Times*, "The Prince in Boston," October 19, 1860.

10. Cornwallis, *Royalty in the New World*, p. 173.

CHAPTER 7

1. Weintraub, *Importance of Being Edward*, p. 107.

2. St. Aubyn, *Edward VII*, p. 63; Weintraub, *Importance of Being Edward*, p. 52.

3. Weintraub, *Importance of Being Edward*, p. 84.

4. Ibid., p. 86.

5. Longford, *Queen Victoria*, p. 44.

6. Presumably it would have been Charles Carrington, a friend of his younger brother.

7. Weintraub, *Importance of Being Edward*, p. 95.

8. Ibid.

9. Ibid.

10. Ibid., p. 96.

11. Ibid.

12. St. Aubyn, *Edward VII*, p. 51.

13. Ibid., near p. 33.

14. Weintraub, *Importance of Being Edward*, p. 102.

15. Ibid., p. 111.

16. St. Aubyn, *Edward VII*, pp. 71–72.

17. Ibid.

CHAPTER 8

1. Van der Kiste, *Queen Victoria's Children*, p. 58.

2. Ibid., p. 63.

3. Weintraub, *Importance of Being Edward*, p. 137.

CHAPTER 9

1. Weintraub, *Importance of Being Edward*, p. 126.
2. Raymond Lamont-Brown, *Alice Keppel and Agnes Keyser: Edward VII's Last Loves* (Thrupp, Stroud, Gloucestershire, Eng.: Sutton, 2005), p. 7.
3. Weintraub, *Importance of Being Edward*, p. 126.
4. St. Aubyn, *Edward VII*, p. 127.
5. Weintraub, *Importance of Being Edward*, p. 142.

CHAPTER 10

1. Lamont-Brown, *Alice Keppel and Agnes Keyser*, p. 18.
2. Brook-Shepherd, *Uncle of Europe*, p. 67.
3. Weintraub, *Importance of Being Edward*, p. 43.
4. Ibid., pp. 207–8.
5. Trevor Mastyn, *Egypt's Belle Époque* (New York: St. Martin's, 2006), p. 105.
6. Georgina Battiscombe, *Queen Alexandra* (Boston: Houghton Mifflin, 1969), p. 130.
7. Middlemas, *Life and Times*, p. 72.
8. St. Aubyn, *Edward VII*, p. 151.
9. Ibid., p. 152.
10. The above account follows John Pearson, *Edward the Rake* (New York and London: Harcourt Brace Jovanovich, 1975).
11. Alphonse Boudard et Romi, *L'âge d'or des maisons closes* (Paris: Albin Michel, 1990), p. 6.
12. Bruce M. Newman, *Fantasy Furniture* (New York: Rizzoli, 1989), p. 145.
13. Mary Blume, *Côte d'Azur: Inventing the French Riviera* (London: Thames and Hudson, 1992), p. 59.
14. Ibid., p. 58.
15. Lamont-Brown *Alice Keppel and Agnes Keyser*, p. 72.
16. St. Aubyn, *Edward VII*, pp. 129–30.

CHAPTER 11

1. Sir Sidney Lee, quoted in Simon Heffer, *Power and Place: The Political Consequences of King Edward VII* (London: Weidenfeld & Nicolson, 1998), p. 7.

CHAPTER 12

1. John C. G. Röhl, *Young Wilhelm* (Cambridge, Eng.: Cambridge University Press, 1998), p. 73.
2. Ibid., p. 67.
3. John C. G. Röhl, *The Kaiser and His Court: Wilhelm II and the Government of Germany* (Cambridge, Eng.: Cambridge University Press, 1994), p. 21.
4. Ibid.
5. Ibid.
6. Ibid., p. 22.
7. Ibid., p. 16.
8. Ibid.
9. Christopher Clark, *Kaiser Wilhelm II* (Harlow, Essex, Eng.: Longman, 2000), p. 4.
10. Ibid., p. 5.
11. Ibid.
12. Ibid.
13. L. C. B. Seaman, *From Vienna to Versailles* (London: Methuen, 1955), p. 96.
14. Röhl, *Young Wilhelm*, p. 432.
15. Ibid., p. xviii.
16. Clark, *Kaiser Wilhelm II*, p. 16.
17. Ibid., p. 17.
18. Ibid., p. 18.
19. Röhl, *Young Wilhelm*, p. 824.

CHAPTER 13

1. Röhl, *Young Wilhelm*, p. 62.
2. Ibid., p. 486. All of the above concerning Willy's sex life comes from Röhl, *Young Wilhelm*, Chapter 18.
3. Clark, *Kaiser Wilhelm II*, p. 35.
4. I follow Clark's account.
5. Clark, *Kaiser Wilhelm II*, p. 125.
6. Ibid.

CHAPTER 14

1. Winston S. Churchill, *The World Crisis 1911–1918* (New York: Free Press, 2005).

2. *Prince Von Bülow Memoirs*, vol. 3, trans. Geoffrey Dunlop and F. A. Voigt (Boston: Little, Brown, 1931), p. 204.

3. Churchill, *World Crisis*, p. 14.

4. Charles S. Campbell, *The Transformation of American Foreign Relations 1865–1900* (New York: Harper & Row, 1976), p. 200.

5. Ibid., p. 209

6. Ibid., p. 211.

7. Walter LaFeber, *The American Search for Opportunity, 1865–1913* (Cambridge, Eng.: Cambridge University Press, 1993), p. 125.

CHAPTER 15

1. Clark, *Kaiser Wilhelm II*, p. 149.

2. Dunlop, *Edward VII*, Chapter 5.

3. Ibid., p. 106.

4. Roderick R. McLean, *Royalty and Diplomacy in Europe, 1890–1914* (Cambridge, Eng.: Cambridge University Press), p. 16.

5. Ibid., p. 27.

6. Clark, *Kaiser Wilhelm II*, p. 100.

7. Ibid., p. 123.

8. Others include the failure to renew the Reinsurance Treaty in 1890 and the decision to go to war in late July 1914.

9. Herman Baron von Eckardstein, quoted in McLean, *Royalty and Diplomacy*, p. 80.

10. Ibid.

11. Clark, *Kaiser Wilhelm II*, p. 10.

12. McLean, *Royalty and Diplomacy*, p. 81.

13. Ibid., p. 84.

14. Ibid., p. 85.

15. Clark, *Kaiser Wilhelm II*, p. 137.

16. Lady Gwendolyn Cecil, *Life of Robert Marquis of Salisbury*, vol. 2, (London: Hodder and Stoughton, 1921), p. 95.

17. Bülow, *Memoirs*, vol. 2, pp. 224–25.

CHAPTER 16

1. Kathleen Dalton, *Theodore Roosevelt: A Strenuous Life* (New York: Vintage, 2004), p. 15.

2. Ibid., p. 26.
3. Ibid., p. 35.
4. Ibid., p. 52.

CHAPTER 17

1. Dalton, *Theodore Roosevelt*, p. 47.
2. Ibid., p. 48.
3. Ibid., p. 68.
4. Ibid., p. 70.
5. Ibid., p. 74.

CHAPTER 18

1. Theodore Roosevelt, *Theodore Roosevelt: An Autobiography* (New York: Charles Scribner's Sons, 1924), pp. 6–7.
2. Ibid., p. 7.
3. Ibid., pp. 14–15.
4. Corinne Roosevelt Robinson, *My Brother Theodore Roosevelt* (New York: Charles Scribner's Sons, 1921), p. 52.
5. Roosevelt, *Autobiography*, p. 19.
6. Letter, Roosevelt to Gilder, August 20, 1903, cited in Joseph Bucklin Bishop, *Theodore Roosevelt and His Time Shown in His Own Letters* (New York: Charles Scribner's Sons, 1920), p. 2.
7. Roosevelt, *Autobiography*, p. 31.
8. Ibid., p. 55.

CHAPTER 19

1. Robinson, *My Brother*, p. 119.
2. Bishop, *Theodore Roosevelt*, p. 19.
3. Ibid., p. 29.
4. Dalton, *Theodore Roosevelt*, p. 95.
5. William C. Widenor, *Henry Cabot Lodge and the Search for an American Foreign Policy* (Berkeley: University of California Press, 1983), p. 2.
6. Ibid., p. 85.
7. Ibid., p. 75.
8. Ibid., p. 89.
9. Ibid., p. 85.

CHAPTER 20

1. Robinson, *My Brother*, p. 123.

2. William Roscoe Thayer, *Theodore Roosevelt: An Intimate Biography* (Boston: Houghton Mifflin, 1919), pp. 58–59.

3. Roosevelt, *Autobiography*, p. 112.

4. Ibid., p. 94.

5. Theodore Roosevelt, *Letters*, vol. 1, ed. Elting E. Morison (Cambridge, Mass.: Harvard University Press, 1951–1954), p. 76.

6. Ibid., p. 73.

7. Thayer, *Intimate Biography*, pp. 60–61.

8. Roosevelt, *Autobiography*, p. 105.

9. Ibid., p. 107.

10. Ibid., pp. 115–16.

11. Roosevelt, *Letters*, p. 82.

12. Letter, cited in Robinson, *My Brother*, p. 138.

13. Roosevelt, *Autobiography*, p. 116.

14. Thayer, *Intimate Biography*, p. 63.

15. Dalton, *Theodore Roosevelt*, p. 95.

CHAPTER 21

1. Dalton, *Theodore Roosevelt*, p. 156.

2. Ibid., p. 156.

3. James Chace and Caleb Carr, *America Invulnerable: The Quest for Absolute Security form 1812 to Star Wars* (New York: Summit, 1988), p. 109.

4. Patricia O'Toole, *The Five of Hearts* (New York: Clarkson Potter, 1990), p. 295.

5. Ibid., p. 299.

CHAPTER 22

1. Though later confused with San Juan Hill, where Roosevelt also fought.

2. Details of battle from Dalton, *Theodore Roosevelt*, p. 174.

3. In 1899, U.S. Vice President Garret Hobart had died in office, thus leaving a vacancy.

CHAPTER 23

1. Dunlop, *Edward VII*, p. 161.

2. Ibid., p. 162.

3. Middlemas, *Life and Times*, p. 104.

4. Jennifer Loach, *Edward VI* (New Haven: Yale University Press, 1999).

5. Dunlop, *Edward VII*, p. 167.

6. Ibid., p. 169.

7. Ibid., p. 171.

8. Middlemas, *Life and Times*, p. 104.

9. Henry James Correspondence, Berg MacM, 1920, pp. 387–88.

10. Henry Adams, *Letters of Henry Adams (1858–1891)*, ed. Worthington Chauncey Ford (Boston: Houghton Mifflin, 1930), p. 379.

11. David Fromkin, *In the Time of the Americans* (New York: Knopf, 1995), p. 28.

12. Mark Twain, *Mark Twain in Eruption* (New York: Harper and Brothers, 1940), pp. 8–9.

CHAPTER 24

1. William N. Tilchin, *Theodore Roosevelt and the British Empire* (New York: St. Martin's, 1997), p. 66.

2. Ibid.

3. A full discussion of the slate that TR had to clean, and of how he did it, is to be found in the works of Professor William N. Tilchin, a leading authority on Roosevelt's foreign policy: in particular, *Theodore Roosevelt and the British Empire*.

4. Howard K. Beale, *Theodore Roosevelt and the Rise of America to World Power* (Baltimore and London: Johns Hopkins Press, 1956), p. 160n.

5. Brands, cited in William N. Tilchin, and Charles E. Neu, *Artists of Power* (Westport, Conn., and London: Praeger, 2006), p. 33.

CHAPTER 25

1. Dunlop, *Edward VII*, p. 140.

2. Zara S. Steiner, *The Foreign Office and Foreign Policy, 1898–1914* (Cambridge, Eng.: Cambridge University Press, 1969,) p. 24.

3. St. Aubyn, *Edward VII*, p. 176.

4. Ibid., pp. 174–76.

5. Steiner, *Foreign Office*, p. 47.

6. Ibid., p. 54.

7. Ibid., p. 71.

8. Francis Bertie is not to be confused with "Bertie," the nickname of the Prince of Wales.

9. Steiner, *Foreign Office,* p. 70.

10. Middlemas, *Life and Times,* p. 160.

11. Dunlop, *Edward VII,* p. 201.

12. C. J. Lowe, and M. L. Dockrill, *The Mirage of Power,* 3 vols. (London and Boston: Routledge & Kegan Paul, 1972), vol. 1, p. 8.

13. Its terms are set forth in the appendix.

CHAPTER 26

1. Wilhelm II, *The Kaiser's Memoirs* (Uckfield, East Sussex: The Naval and Military Press, 2005), p. 312.

2. Dunlop, *Edward VII,* p. 234.

3. Ibid., p. 239 for the message, which in part is paraphrased.

4. Ibid., p. 255.

5. See Douglas Porch, *The Conquest of Morocco* (New York: Fromm, 1986), p. 145 et seq., for Algeciras.

6. Porch, p. 145.

7. Bülow, *Memoirs,* vol. II, p. 3.

8. Ibid.

CHAPTER 27

1. Bülow, *Memoirs.*

2. After ninety years, the French conquest of Morocco would be completed in 1934.

3. Beale, *Theodore Roosevelt,* p. 359.

4. Ibid.

5. Tilchin, *Theodore Roosevelt,* p. 86.

6. Ibid., p. 87.

CHAPTER 28

1. Dunlop, *Edward VII,* p. 254.

2. Beale, *Theodore Roosevelt,* p. 377.

3. Wilhelm II, *Memoirs,* pp. 115–16.

4. Theodore Roosevelt Papers. Library of Congress. Letter dated April 25, 1906, to King Edward VII.

5. A. J. P. Taylor, *Englishmen and Others* (London: Hamish Hamilton, 1952), p. 88.

CHAPTER 29

1. Steiner, *Foreign Office*, p. 109.

2. George Monger, *The End of Isolation: British Foreign Policy 1900–1907* (London: Nelson, 1963), p. 262.

3. Ibid., pp. 262–63.

4. Ibid., p. 263.

5. Ibid.

6. Middlemas, *Life and Times*, p. 163.

CHAPTER 30

1. A story told in Fromkin, *In the Time of the Americans.*

2. Barbara Tuchman, *The Guns of August* (New York: Dell, 1962), p. 15.

3. Ibid.

4. Ibid.

5. Dunlop, *Edward VII*, p. 286.

CHAPTER 31

1. David Fromkin, *Europe's Last Summer* (New York: Knopf, 2004), p. 78.

APPENDIX

1. Lowe and Dockrill, *Mirage of Power.*

BIBLIOGRAPHY

ADAMS, FRANCIS A. *Theodore Roosevelt: His Policies, His Enemies, His Friends.* New York: Wintemute-Sawyer Publishing Company, 1909.

ADAMS, HENRY. *Letters of Henry Adams (1858–1891).* Ed. Worthington Chauncey Ford. Boston: Houghton Mifflin, 1930.

ADLER, LAURA. *La Vie Quotidienne dans les Maisons Closes 1830–1930.* 4 vols. Paris: Hachette, 1990.

ALBERTINI, LUIGI. *The Origins of the War of 1914.* 3 vols. London: Oxford University Press, 1952.

ALLFREY, ANTHONY. *Edward VII and His Jewish Court.* London: Weidenfeld & Nicolson, 1991.

ANDREW, CHRISTOPHER. *Théophile Delcassé and the Making of the Entente Cordiale.* New York: St. Martin's, 1968.

BATTISCOMBE, GEORGINA. *Queen Alexandra.* Boston: Houghton Mifflin, 1969.

BEALE, HOWARD K. *Theodore Roosevelt and the Rise of America to World Power.* Baltimore and London: Johns Hopkins Press, 1956.

BISHOP, JOSEPH BUCKLIN. *Theodore Roosevelt and His Time Shown in His Own Letters.* New York: Charles Scribner's Sons, 1920.

BLUME, MARY. *Côte d'Azur: Inventing the French Riviera.* London: Thames and Hudson, 1992.

BOUDARD, ALPHONSE, ET ROMI. *L'âge d'or des maisons closes.* Paris: Albin Michel, 1990.

BRANDS, H. W. *T.R.: The Last Romantic.* New York: Basic Books, 1997.

BROOK-SHEPHERD, GORDON. *Uncle of Europe: The Social and Diplomatic Life of Edward VII.* New York and London: Harcourt Brace Jovanovich, 1975.

BÜLOW, PRINCE VON. *Memoirs.* 4 vols. Trans. Geoffrey Dunlop and F. A. Voigt. Boston: Little, Brown, 1931.

CAMPBELL, CHARLES S. *The Transformation of American Foreign Relations 1865–1900*. New York: Harper & Row, 1976.

CECIL, LADY GWENDOLEN. *Life of Robert Marquis of Salisbury*. 4 vols. London: Hodder and Stoughton, 1921.

CHACE, JAMES, AND CALEB CARR. *America Invulnerable: The Quest for Absolute Security from 1812 to Star Wars*. New York: Summit, 1988.

CHURCHILL, WINSTON S. *The World Crisis 1911–1918*. New York: The Free Press, 2005.

CLARK, CHRISTOPHER. *Kaiser Wilhelm II*. Harlow, Essex, Eng.: Longman, 2000.

CORNWALLIS, KINAHAN. *Royalty in the New World—or—The Prince of Wales in America*. New York: Doolard, 1860.

CRAIG, GORDON A. *Germany 1866–1945*. New York: Oxford University Press, 1978.

DALTON, KATHLEEN. *Theodore Roosevelt: A Strenuous Life*. New York: Vintage, 2004.

D'ARJUZON, ANTOINE. *Edouard VII*. France: Perrin, 2004.

DUNLOP, IAN. *Edward VII and the Entente Cordiale*. London: Constable, 2004.

FROMKIN, DAVID. *Europe's Last Summer*. New York: Knopf, 2004.

———. *In the Time of the Americans*. New York: Knopf, 1995.

GEOFFROY, CHRISTINE. *Les Coulisses de l'Entente Cordiale*. Paris: Grasset, 2004.

HALLER, JOHANNES. *Philip Eulenburg: The Kaiser's Friend*. 2 vols. Trans. Ethel Colburn Mayne. New York: Knopf, 1930.

HAYNE, M. B. *The French Foreign Office and the Origins of the First World War 1898–1914*. Oxford: Clarendon Press, 1993.

HEFFER, SIMON. *Power and Place: The Political Consequences of King Edward VII*. London: Weidenfeld & Nicolson, 1998.

HIBBERT, CHRISTOPHER. *Edward VII: A Portrait*. London: Allen Lane, 1976.

HUGHES, MICHAEL. *Diplomacy Before the Russian Revolution: Britain, Russia, and the Old Diplomacy, 1894–1917*. New York: St. Martin's, 2000.

JAMES, HENRY. *The Correspondence of Henry James and Henry Adams, 1877–1914*. Ed. George Monteiro. Baton Rouge: Louisiana State University Press, 1992.

JAMES, WILLIAM. *William and Henry James: Selected Letters*. Ed. John M. McDermott. Charlottesville: University Press of Virginia, 1997.

JULLIAN, PHILIPPE. *Edward and the Edwardians*. Trans. Peter Dawnay. New York: Viking, 1967.

JUSSERAND, JEAN-JULES. *What Me Befell*. Boston: Houghton Mifflin, 1933.

KENNAN, GEORGE F. *The Fateful Alliance: France, Russia, and the Coming of the First World War*. New York: Pantheon, 1984.

KENNEDY, PAUL M. *The Rise of the Anglo-German Antagonism 1860–1914*. London: George Allen & Unwin, 1980.

LAFEBER, WALTER. *The Cambridge History of American Foreign Relations*. 4 vols. Vol. II, *The American Search for Opportunity, 1865–1913*. Cambridge, Eng.: Cambridge University Press, 1993.

LAMONT-BROWN, RAYMOND. *Alice Keppel and Agnes Keyser: Edward VII's Last Loves*. Thrupp, Stroud, Gloucestershire, Eng.: Sutton, 2005.

LANGER, WILLIAM L. *The Diplomacy of Imperialism 1890–1902*. New York: Knopf, 1951.

———. *European Alliances and Alignments, 1871–1890*. New York: Knopf, 1956.

LEE, SIR SIDNEY. *King Edward VII*. 2 vols. New York: Macmillan, 1925.

LONGFORD, ELIZABETH. *Queen Victoria*. Thrupp, Stroud, Gloucestershire, Eng.: Sutton, 2005.

LOWE, C. J., AND M. L. DOCKRILL. *The Mirage of Power*. 3 vols. London and Boston: Routledge & Kegan Paul, 1972.

MAGNUS, PHILIP. *King Edward the Seventh*. New York: Dutton, 1964.

MARSH, PETER T. *Joseph Chamberlain: Entrepreneur in Politics*. New Haven and London: Yale University Press, 1994.

MAUROIS, ANDRÉ. *King Edward VII and His Times*. Trans. Hamish Miles. London: Cassell, 1933.

MAYER, MARTIN. *Geheime Diplomatie und Öffentliche Meinung*. Dusseldorf: Droste, 2002.

MCLEAN, RODERICK R. *Royalty and Diplomacy in Europe, 1890–1914*. Cambridge, Eng.: Cambridge University Press.

MIDDLEMAS, KEITH. *The Life and Times of Edward VII*. Garden City, N.Y.: Doubleday, 1972.

MONGER, GEORGE. *The End of Isolation: British Foreign Policy 1900–1907*. London: Nelson, 1963.

MORRIS, THEODORE. *The Rise of Theodore Roosevelt*. New York: Modern Library, 1979.

————. *Theodore Rex.* New York: Modern Library, 2001.

MORTON, FREDERIC. *A Nervous Splendor: Vienna 1888–1889.* New York: Penguin, 1979.

MOSTYN, TREVOR. *Egypt's Belle Epoque: Cairo and the Age of the Hedonists.* London and New York: Tauris, 2006.

"MR. ROOSEVELT'S CREED," *New York Times,* October 19, 1884.

NEVINS, ALLAN. *Henry White: Thirty Years of American Diplomacy.* New York: Harper, 1930.

NEWMAN, BRUCE M. *Fantasy Furniture.* New York: Rizzoli, 1989.

O'TOOLE, PATRICIA. *The Five of Hearts.* New York: Clarkson Potter, 1990.

PAKENHAM, THOMAS. *The Boer War.* New York: Random House, 1979.

PEARSON, JOHN. *Edward the Rake.* New York and London: Harcourt Brace Jovanovich, 1975.

PERKINS, BRADFORD. *The Great Rapprochement: England and the United States, 1895–1914.* New York: Atheneum, 1968.

PLUMB, J. H. *England in the Eighteenth Century.* Baltimore: Penguin, 1950.

————. *The First Four Georges.* London: Collins, 1956.

PORCH, DOUGLAS. *The Conquest of Morocco.* New York: Fromm, 1986.

PRINGLE, HENRY F. *The Kaiser and His Court: Wilhelm II and the Government of Germany.* Cambridge, Eng.: Cambridge University Press, 1994.

————. *Theodore Roosevelt: A Biography.* New York: Harcourt, Brace & World, 1931.

ROBINSON, CORINNE ROOSEVELT. *My Brother Theodore Roosevelt.* New York: Charles Scribner's Sons, 1921.

RÖHL, JOHN C. G. *The Kaiser and His Court: Wilhelm II and the Government of Germany.* Cambridge, Eng.: Cambridge University Press, 1994.

————. *Wilhelm II: The Kaiser's Personal Monarchy, 1888–1900.* Cambridge, Eng.: Cambridge University Press, 2004.

————. *Young Wilhelm.* Cambridge, Eng.: Cambridge University Press, 1998.

ROOSEVELT, THEODORE. *Theodore Roosevelt: An Autobiography.* New York: Charles Scribner's Sons, 1924.

————. *Letters.* Ed. Elting E. Morison. Cambridge, Mass.: Harvard University Press, 1951–1954.

SAMUELS, ERNEST. *Henry Adams.* Cambridge, Mass., and London: Harvard University Press, 1989.

SCHORSKE, CARL E. *Fin-de-Siècle Vienna: Politics and Culture.* New York: Knopf, 1980.

SEAMAN, L. C. B. *From Vienna to Versailles.* London: Methuen, 1955.

SKINNER, CORNELIA OTIS. *Elegant Wits and Grand Horizontals.* Boston: Houghton Mifflin, 1962.

ST. AUBYN, GILES. *Edward VII: Prince and King.* New York: Atheneum, 1979.

STEINER, ZARA S. *The Foreign Office and Foreign Policy, 1898–1914.* Cambridge, Eng.: Cambridge University Press, 1969.

STRACHEY, LYTTON. *Queen Victoria.* London: Chatto and Windus, 1948.

TARDIEU, ANDRÉ. *La Conférence d'Algésiras: Histoire Diplomatique de la Crise Marocaine (15 janvier–7 avril 1906).* Paris: Alcan, 1907.

TAYLOR, A. J. P. *Englishmen and Others.* London: Hamish Hamilton, 1956.

———. *From the Boer War to the Cold War: Essays on Twentieth-Century Europe.* London: Penguin, 1995.

———. *Rumours of War.* London: Hamish Hamilton, 1952.

———. *The Struggle for Mastery in Europe 1848–1918.* Oxford: Clarendon Press, 1954.

THAYER, WILLIAM ROSCOE. *John Hay.* Boston: Houghton Mifflin, 1915.

———. *Theodore Roosevelt: An Intimate Biography.* Boston: Houghton Mifflin, 1919.

TILCHIN, WILLIAM N. *Theodore Roosevelt and the British Empire.* New York: St. Martin's, 1997.

TILCHIN, WILLIAM N., AND CHARLES E. NEU. *Artists of Power.* Westport, Conn., and London: Praeger, 2006.

TUCHMAN, BARBARA. *The Guns of August.* New York: Dell, 1962.

TWAIN, MARK. *Mark Twain in Eruption.* New York: Harper and Brothers, 1940.

VAN DER KISTE, JOHN. *Queen Victoria's Children.* Thrupp, Stroud, Gloucestershire, Eng.: Sutton, 2003.

WEBER, EUGEN. *France: Fin de Siecle.* Cambridge, Mass., and London: Harvard University Press, 1986.

WEINTRAUB, STANLEY. *The Importance of Being Edward: King in Waiting 1841–1901.* London: John Murray, 2000.

WIDENOR, WILLIAM C. *Henry Cabot Lodge and the Search for an American Foreign Policy.* Berkeley: University of California Press, 1983.

WILHELM II. *The Kaiser's Memoirs.* Uckfield, East Sussex: The Naval and Military Press, 2005.

WOODHAM-SMITH, CECIL. *Queen Victoria.* New York: Knopf, 1972.

ZELDIN, THEODORE. *France, 1848–1945.* 2 vols. Oxford: Clarendon Press, 1973.

Internet Resources

GRIESSMAN, GENE. *The Lincoln-Roosevelt Connection.* http://www.teddyleads. com/library/LincolnRooseveltconnection.pdf (accessed June 12, 2007).

BLAKE, NELSON MANFRED. "Ambassadors to the Court of Theodore Roosevelt." *American Heritage Magazine,* February 1956, Vol. 7(2). http:// www.americanheritage.com/articles/magazine/ah/1956/2/1956220. shtml

TWAIN, MARK. *The Letters of Mark Twain, Complete.* http://www.fullbooks. com/The-Letters-Of-Mark-Twain-Complete.html

INDEX

ABOUT THE AUTHOR

DAVID FROMKIN is University Professor, Professor of International Relations, of History, and of Law at Boston University. He served for three years as Chairman of the Department of International Relations and Director of the Center for International Relations. He has been a member of the Council on Foreign Relations since 1976. His shorter pieces have appeared in *Foreign Affairs,* the *New York Times,* and other publications. He is the author of seven books, including: *The Question of Government: An Inquiry into the breakdown of Modern Political Systems* (1975), *The Independence of Nations* (1981), *In the Time of the Americans: FDR, Truman, Eisenhower, Marshall, MacArthur, the Generation That Changed America's Role in the World* (1995). His 1989 book, *A Peace to End All Peace: Creating the Modern Middle East 1914–1922* (1989), was a national bestseller, was chosen by the editors of the *New York Times Book Review* as one of the dozen best books of the year, and was short-listed for the Pulitzer Prize. His most recent book, published in March 2004, is *Europe's Last Summer: Who Started the Great War in 1914?*